DATE DUE

OC 31 '96			
DE 18 '96			
MY 14 '97			
OC 2 '97			
DE 15 '97			
MY 26 98			
AP 24 00			
DE 9 02			
DE 14 '04			
OC 29 12			
SE 24 '15			

DEMCO 38-296

The Legal System

OPPOSING VIEWPOINTS®

Other Books of Related Interest:

Opposing Viewpoints Series

America's Prisons
America's Victims
Child Abuse
Crime and Criminals
Criminal Justice
The Death Penalty
Feminism
Gangs
Homosexuality
Mental Illness
Race Relations
Social Justice
Violence
War on Drugs

Current Controversies

The Abortion Controversy
Drug Trafficking
Ethics
Gambling
Gun Control
Hate Crimes
Illegal Immigration
Police Brutality
Sexual Harassment
Violence Against Women
Youth Violence

At Issue Series

Business Ethics
Immigration Policy
Legalizing Drugs
Policing the Police

The Legal System

OPPOSING VIEWPOINTS®

David Bender & Bruno Leone, *Series Editors*

Tamara L. Roleff, *Book Editor*

OPPOSING
VIEWPOINTS®
SERIES

Greenhaven Press, Inc., San Diego, CA

:d or used in any form or by
r otherwise, including, but
or any information storage
ritten permission from the

Greenhaven Press, Inc.
PO Box 289009
San Diego, CA 92198-9009

Library of Congress Cataloging-in-Publication Data

The legal system : opposing viewpoints / Tamara L. Roleff, book
    editor.
        p.   cm. — (Opposing viewpoints series)
    Includes bibliographical references and index.
    ISBN 1-56510-405-6 (lib. : alk. paper). —
ISBN 1-56510-404-8 (pbk. bdg. : alk. paper)
    1. Justice, Administration of—United States. 2. Jury—United
States. 3. Law—United States. I. Roleff, Tamara L., 1959–   .
II. Series: Opposing viewpoints series (Unnumbered)
KF8700.L39 1996
347.73—dc20   95-49643
[347.307]   CIP

"Congress shall make no law . . . abridging the freedom of speech, or of the press."

First Amendment to the U.S. Constitution

The basic foundation of our democracy is the First Amendment guarantee of freedom of expression. The Opposing Viewpoints Series is dedicated to the concept of this basic freedom and the idea that it is more important to practice it than to enshrine it.

Contents

Chapter 3: Is There a Litigation Explosion?

Chapter 4: Is the Criminal Justice System Fair?

Chapter 5: How Do the Media Affect the Legal System?

Why Consider Opposing Viewpoints?

"The only way in which a human being can make some approach to knowing the whole of a subject is by hearing what can be said about it by persons of every variety of opinion and studying all modes in which it can be looked at by every character of mind. No wise man ever acquired his wisdom in any mode but this."

John Stuart Mill

In our media-intensive culture it is not difficult to find differing opinions. Thousands of newspapers and magazines and dozens of radio and television talk shows resound with differing points of view. The difficulty lies in deciding which opinion to agree with and which "experts" seem the most credible. The more inundated we become with differing opinions and claims, the more essential it is to hone critical reading and thinking skills to evaluate these ideas. Opposing Viewpoints books address this problem directly by presenting stimulating debates that can be used to enhance and teach these skills. The varied opinions contained in each book examine many different aspects of a single issue. While examining these conveniently edited opposing views, readers can develop critical thinking skills such as the ability to compare and contrast authors' credibility, facts, argumentation styles, use of persuasive techniques, and other stylistic tools. In short, the Opposing Viewpoints Series is an ideal way to attain the higher-level thinking and reading skills so essential in a culture of diverse and contradictory opinions.

In addition to providing a tool for critical thinking, Opposing Viewpoints books challenge readers to question their own strongly held opinions and assumptions. Most people form their opinions on the basis of upbringing, peer pressure, and personal, cultural, or professional bias. By reading carefully balanced opposing views, readers must directly confront new ideas as well as the opinions of those with whom they disagree. This is not to simplistically argue that everyone who reads opposing views will—or should—change his or her opinion. Instead, the series enhances readers' depth of understanding of their own views by encouraging confrontation with opposing ideas. Careful examination of others' views can lead to the readers' understanding of the logical inconsistencies in their own opinions, perspective on why they hold an opinion, and the consideration of the possibility that their opinion requires further evaluation.

Evaluating Other Opinions

To ensure that this type of examination occurs, Opposing Viewpoints books present all types of opinions. Prominent spokespeople on different sides of each issue as well as well-known professionals from many disciplines challenge the reader. An additional goal of the series is to provide a forum for other, less known, or even unpopular viewpoints. The opinion of an ordinary person who has had to make the decision to cut off life support from a terminally ill relative, for example, may be just as valuable and provide just as much insight as a medical ethicist's professional opinion. The editors have two additional purposes in including these less known views. One, the editors encourage readers to respect others' opinions—even when not enhanced by professional credibility. It is only by reading or listening to and objectively evaluating others' ideas that one can determine whether they are worthy of consideration. Two, the inclusion of such viewpoints encourages the important critical thinking skill of objectively evaluating an author's credentials and bias. This evaluation will illuminate an author's reasons for taking a particular stance on an issue and will aid in readers' evaluation of the author's ideas.

As series editors of the Opposing Viewpoints Series, it is our hope that these books will give readers a deeper understanding of the issues debated and an appreciation of the complexity of even seemingly simple issues when good and honest people disagree. This awareness is particularly important in a democratic society such as ours in which people enter into public debate to determine the common good. Those with whom one disagrees should not be regarded as enemies but rather as people whose views deserve careful examination and may shed light on one's own.

Thomas Jefferson once said that "difference of opinion leads to inquiry, and inquiry to truth." Jefferson, a broadly educated man, argued that "if a nation expects to be ignorant and free . . . it expects what never was and never will be." As individuals and as a nation, it is imperative that we consider the opinions of others and examine them with skill and discernment. The Opposing Viewpoints Series is intended to help readers achieve this goal.

David L. Bender & Bruno Leone,
Series Editors

Introduction

"*The issue of cameras in the courts has come under intense scrutiny.*"

Steven Brill

The murders of O.J. Simpson's ex-wife Nicole and her friend Ronald Goldman attracted intense media attention from the minute their bodies were found on June 12, 1994, in the tony Los Angeles neighborhood of Brentwood, California. Five days later, millions of television viewers watched as police followed Simpson in his white Ford Bronco on Los Angeles freeways in a low-speed chase. About 1.5 million homes tuned in to watch the prosecution's opening arguments on January 24, 1995. But the biggest event during the trial was the reading of the verdict on October 3, 1995. Four American television broadcast networks, six national cable channels, and numerous foreign networks covered the dramatic announcement live. A viewing audience of about 108 million Americans—about 91 percent of those watching TV at the time—tuned in to hear Simpson's jury pronounce him not guilty of the murders. Yet despite, or perhaps because of, the extreme interest in Simpson's trial, television's role in the courts has become the subject of intense debate.

Opponents of televised trials insist that cameras in the courtroom miseducate the public about America's legal system. They claim that most people who watch televised trials are drawn to atypical, high-profile cases. These cases give the public misleading views of the justice system, argues author and former criminal defense lawyer Wendy Kaminer. The majority of defendants are not even tried, she maintains, but plea bargain their way through the system.

Critics also charge that cameras in the courtroom lead to a circus atmosphere surrounding the trial. Anti-camera forces cite the "media circus" that emerged during Simpson's pretrial hearing, which included actors re-enacting scenes described in the hearing, an "O.J.-ometer" that measured how well the trial was going every day for Simpson, and news and talk shows that featured obscure guests and topics related to the Simpson trial to increase their ratings points.

Opponents of cameras in the courtroom also disagree with those who claim that banning televised coverage compromises

12

the public's right to know. Joan Weber, a San Diego Superior Court judge, argues that keeping cameras out of the courtroom does not limit the public's access to the courtroom. She contends that high-profile cases, such as the Simpson trial, was "on the front page of every major newspaper in this country" and was "reported on every TV newscast every night." Others maintain that journalists are able to present the public with a better perspective of a trial. News anchor Ted Koppel argues that journalists, who are more knowledgeable about a particular case than the average viewer, can provide the public with a more informative record of events than that supplied by a camera alone.

Perhaps the most frequently heard argument against televising trials is the contention that cameras change the behavior of all the participants involved in the trial—the lawyers, the judge, the witnesses, and the jurors. Opponents claim witnesses may be frightened about being televised or may change their testimony after watching another witness testify on TV; jurors may be corrupted by the prospect of a few minutes of fame and invitations to appear on talk shows after a televised trial; and lawyers and judges may play to the camera. "No one can deny that both prosecution and defense teams were much more theatrical and performance-oriented because the camera was in that courtroom," maintains Carol LeBeau, a television news anchor in San Diego, referring to the Simpson trial. Paul Pringle of the Copley News Service compared the behavior of Lance Ito, the California Superior Court judge who presided over the Simpson trial, to that of a game-show host:

> From Day One, he mugged, he smiled, he cracked jokes for the TV audience. He decorated the courtroom with floral arrangements from well-wishers. He extended birthday wishes from the bench to a particularly loyal viewer.

Proponents of televising trials agree that cameras may change the behavior of some participants—but for the better. Lawyers and judges are on their best behavior when they know they will be on camera, claims attorney Ronald Goldfarb:

> Experienced trial lawyers know that judges are likely to be more autocratic and idiosyncratic when the public isn't looking. Aren't people on their best behavior when they are being watched? And if not, before it is possible to correct misbehavior, it must be known.

Therefore, Goldfarb concludes, televising trials, "warts and all," may lead to public understanding of an unpopular verdict or to demands that the American judicial system be reformed.

As to charges that lawyers grandstand when trials are televised, advocates of cameras in the courtroom argue that such claims are baseless. Attorneys have a long tradition of theatrical behavior in notorious cases, asserts Floyd Abrams, a lawyer and professor of First Amendment issues at the Columbia University Graduate School of Journalism. The untelevised trials of Sacco and Vanzetti, Ethel and Julius Rosenberg, and John Gotti were all filled with grandstanding lawyers and the type of behavior that is routinely blamed on television cameras, he maintains. Abrams contends that if the lengthy trials of Charles Manson (nine months) and the California Hillside Strangler (twenty-three months) had been televised, television cameras would have been blamed for their long duration as well.

Those who support the role of cameras in the courtroom maintain that television viewers should not be forced to rely on a reporter's assessment of what happens in the courtroom. Judge Ito defends the role of cameras in his courtroom:

> The problem with not having a camera is that one must trust the evaluation and analysis of a reporter who's telling you what occurred in the courtroom. Any time you allow somebody to report an event, you have to take into consideration the filtering effect of that person's own biases. Whereas if you have a camera in the courtroom, there's no filtering. What you see is what's there.

Other proponents of cameras in the courtroom maintain that televising trials educates the public. They contend that by watching trials, television viewers learn about legal rules, such as probable cause, suppression of evidence, and reasonable doubt, and about different institutions and procedures, including the jury system, the adversary system, the prosecution and defense, and police procedures. Steven Brill, founder of the cable channel Court TV, argues that televising trials benefits the public. "Instead of soap operas and freak-of-the-day talk shows, we [get] a riveting lesson about what our Constitution allows and doesn't allow the police to do."

Brill also insists that the three-ring circus atmosphere that so many opponents of televised trials complain about is not due to an unobtrusive camera in the courtroom. He contends that the media circus is the result of media activities outside the courtroom. The one small camera mounted inconspicuously on a wall in the courtroom is merely a mirror of what goes on inside the courtroom, he argues.

The role of the media in the courtroom is just one of the issues debated in *The Legal System: Opposing Viewpoints*, which contains the following chapters: Does the Jury System Work? Does the Civil Justice System Need Reform? Is There a Litigation Explosion? Is the Criminal Justice System Fair? How Do the Media Affect the Legal System? Whether Americans consider the legal system the best possible method of determining guilt or innocence or a system drastically in need of reform, this anthology can provide a better understanding of the issues involved.

Does the Jury System Work?

The
Legal
System

Chapter Preface

In a country where the majority rules in Congress, elections, government, and even the U.S. Supreme Court, the American jury system stands out for its requirement of unanimous verdicts. Yet two states—Oregon and Louisiana—allow juries to return with majority verdicts in noncapital felony cases. The U.S. Supreme Court sustained majority verdicts as constitutional in 1972 in the cases of *Apodaca v. Oregon* and *Johnson v. Louisiana*. In its rulings, the Supreme Court found that majority verdicts were just as fair to defendants as unanimous verdicts.

Proponents of majority verdicts argue that this approach is superior to the use of unanimous verdicts in ensuring that justice is served. Jacob Tanzer, a Portland, Oregon, lawyer who argued the issue before the Supreme Court, contends that unanimous verdicts are frequently the results of compromises, in which, for example, rapists or armed robbers are often convicted only of the lesser charge of assault. "When jurors can vote their minds without the need to compromise, the verdict better reflects the truth," he maintains. Tanzer argues that when a majority jury deliberates, the dissenters' views are listened to until the jury either comes to a unanimous agreement or has exhausted all possibilities of doing so. "Majorities tend to return non-unanimous verdicts only when they believe that further discussion is futile," he writes.

Others contend that majority verdicts undermine justice. Jeffrey Abramson, in his book *We, the Jury*, maintains that jurors who are allowed to give a majority verdict tend to "stop . . . the deliberations when the required number [is] reached." He cites studies that show that nationally, juries are hung by one or two jurors in only 2.4 percent of all trials; yet in Oregon, which allows 10-2 verdicts, 25 percent of all verdicts reached are 10-2 or 11-1. After juries reach the required number of votes, Abramson argues, they have "polite" debate, in which the jurors deign to listen to opposing arguments for a few more minutes before rendering their verdict, rather than "robust" debate, in which they actively try to persuade the dissenters to change their votes.

Most lawyers, judges, and legal experts agree that the jury system could be improved. Reforms most often cited include allowing jurors to take notes during a trial, permitting them to ask questions of the witnesses, and having the judge instruct the jurors in points of law before testimony begins rather than at the end of the trial. Some reformers advocate abolishing the jury system altogether. The viewpoints in the following chapter debate whether the jury system is still necessary, what powers should be given to the jury, and whether juries should be allowed to talk about their deliberations with the press.

> "The criminal jury system, right or wrong, is still one of our greatest and most characteristically American institutions."

The Criminal Jury System Is Effective

Barbara Allen Babcock

Although juries may sometimes make mistakes when deciding their verdicts, Barbara Allen Babcock argues in the following viewpoint, that is not reason enough to reform the criminal jury system. For every jury that gives a wrong verdict, there are hundreds of juries that render the correct verdict, she maintains. Furthermore, Babcock contends that reforms to the jury system may have unintended consequences: Changing any of the jury's fundamental features may harm rather than improve the system. The jury's basic attributes guarantee that the accused is protected from the state, she asserts, making the criminal jury system an essential part of American democracy. Babcock is a law professor at Stanford University and a former assistant attorney general under the Carter administration.

As you read, consider the following questions:

1. What are the historical attributes of the jury, in the author's view?
2. According to Babcock, what has been the unintended consequence of disallowing lawyers to question potential jurors?
3. In what ways can the basic attributes of the criminal jury be preserved, in Babcock's opinion?

Barbara Allen Babcock, "Protect the Jury System, Judge Was the Problem," *Los Angeles Times*, October 8, 1995. Reprinted by permission of the author.

"I personally would have a reasonable doubt, but it's true there is overwhelming evidence that he is possibly guilty."

This statement by an African-American man, interviewed on TV shortly before the verdict [was announced] in the O.J. Simpson double-murder trial in October 1995, reveals the tension inherent in our jury system. "Overwhelming evidence" may lead only to the "possibility" of guilt, and in its face, the jury may still entertain sufficient reservations to acquit.

Juries may also make mistakes, may be swayed by passion, prejudice and sympathy to acquit a guilty person; may misread the evidence, or misconstrue their duty. The first Simpson jurors to speak out seem to be saying that they took quite literally the judge's instruction that they might discount totally the evidence of police officers who lied in some respects. In a sense, they may have become the enforcers of exclusionary rules that many judges no longer follow. Even as individual jurors come forward, however, we are not likely to fully understand the dynamics that led to Simpson's acquittal.

But all who think, as I do, that this verdict is wrong, should not turn their frustration and anger on the criminal jury system itself. Far worse than letting a guilty man go free would be losing faith in, or working fundamental changes on, this most American of institutions.

Even before the Simpson verdicts were in . . . there were legislative moves afoot in California: to do away with the unanimity requirement; to reduce the number of jurors; to abolish peremptory challenges. There are two basic problems with these proposals: First, they rest on a faulty premise that the jury system is broken, and, second, they have the potential to change its operation profoundly in unpredictable ways.

The Price of Liberty

That the jury may make mistakes—or may express through its verdict community sentiment that is, at best, extra-legal—is part of the system, part of the price we pay to have a judgment of the people before we deprive anyone of all liberty. We have always, from the founding of the republic, been willing to sustain the risk that a jury will be wrong. Nothing in the Simpson verdicts changes that.

For every jury that goes awry, there are a hundred that do the right thing. Lawyers on both sides of the criminal system, former jurors and most academics who have studied juries, attest to this. I believe in juries based on my experience as a young lawyer, when I tried many cases—losing some and winning others, representing mostly African American men before mostly African American juries in Washington.

Though losing a verdict is one of life's crushing blows, in vir-

18

tually all cases I saw close up, the jury made a correct, and wise, decision. More than occasionally, I found that jurors who started with one predisposition—sometimes ones I had chosen because I discerned it—changed their minds through the deliberations.

But no jury in my experience was so mistreated and abused as the Simpson jury. Indeed, it might well be that the mismanagement of the jury helped produce the acquittal. This is the second reason why this case should not be an occasion for sweeping changes: the law of unintended consequences.

Proposed Reforms Are Misguided

The ultimate danger of the public's disgust with the Simpson trial is that it will fuel efforts to change the legal system and that these will be misdirected because the case is truly unique. Also, reforms inspired by the Simpson case are likely to be misguided because much of the criticism focuses on minor issues and not the real problems facing the criminal justice system. . . .

[The Simpson case] already has inspired legislation that unconstitutionally limits speech by witnesses and jurors. It has caused efforts to restrict the ability of attorneys to speak to the press. It is partially responsible for proposals to allow non-unanimous jury verdicts in criminal cases. Yet none of these so-called reforms deals with real problems or the serious failings in the legal system.

Erwin Chemerinsky, *Los Angeles Times*, August 18, 1995.

We do not know what makes juries work well most of the time—which feature is necessary to proper functioning. The jury comes with certain historical attributes: the mystical number 12; the absolute power, without accountability, to acquit; the judicial filtering of the evidence they will hear; the absence of merit-type qualifications of education or training for service; the requirement that they engage each other to the point of total agreement. No one knows which, if any, of these is essential to the integrity of the institution.

We do know, however, that a jury should be a group put together once in time for a single purpose, that it should be composed of strangers, who know each other only through their deliberations.

This fundamental feature was violated in the Simpson case by a star-struck judge who lost control of the situation. Judge Lance A. Ito caused the jury to spend many hours waiting while he heard and reheard lawyers' arguments, took time off to engage celebrities and, through it all, patronized the jurors—conveying by his tone and manner that their time was not important. He should have taken drastic measures to move the trial along—for example, he might have heard motions in the evenings, and held court on Saturdays. Instead, by his leisurely approach, he violated the very premises of the jury and permitted the possibility that they would become a little band with their own agenda.

Legal Statutes and Their Consequences

But Ito, like the judges in most states, was largely on his own in deciding how to deal with this jury. The statutes, and common law, on the selection, care and instruction of juries are a hodgepodge of piecemeal rules—some adopted in reaction to unpopular verdicts—without concern for how the system, as a whole, will be affected. The most recent addition, for instance, imposed by initiative, removed the right of lawyers to question potential jurors. By the report of both prosecutors and defenders, the unintended consequence of this law has been a dramatic increase in hung juries—because lawyers on both sides are unable to uncover through follow-up questions and direct contact, those who may prove to be unreasoning outliers in jury deliberation.

Rather than such reactive legislation, a comprehensive statute that preserved the jury's basic attributes would be a good outcome of the Simpson verdicts. Such a statute should include, for example, provisions regularizing selection practices, including juror questionnaires tailored to the facts of the individual cases; provision for expedited procedures in cases of sequestration, and for more reasonable compensation and treatment of jurors.

Meanwhile, whether or not we agree with the Simpson verdict, all should accept and respect it. The criminal jury system, right or wrong, is still one of our greatest and most characteristically American institutions. Like universal suffrage—a vote for every citizen regardless of class, race or gender—the jury drawn from the community with absolute power to protect the accused from the state is fundamental to our democracy.

"The American jury system does not work to free the innocent and punish the guilty in an efficient and humane manner. It never has."

The Criminal Jury System Should Be Reformed

Michael Lind

The American criminal jury system, which is derived from English common law, requires that the accused be tried by a jury of twelve peers. However, many European nations, which inherited their criminal justice system from Roman civil law, provide for a jury of professional and lay judges—not a jury of peers—in criminal trials. Michael Lind, a senior editor for the *New Republic* magazine, argues in the following viewpoint that the American common-law jury of peers does not work as well as the civil-law jury of judges. The American criminal jury trial is based on primitive and outdated concepts of law that are no longer valid in modern civilized society, he maintains. The American jury system is in need of drastic reform, Lind contends—reform that may require Americans to abandon some established legal traditions and adopt policies from other countries.

As you read, consider the following questions:

1. How is the American criminal jury system similar to trial by combat and torture, in the author's view?
2. Why is a civil-law jury better than a common-law jury, in Lind's opinion?
3. How might dissatisfaction with a common-law jury verdict result in vigilantism, according to Lind?

Michael Lind, "Jury Dismissed," *New Republic*, October 23, 1995. Reprinted by permission of the *New Republic*; ©1995 by The New Republic, Inc.

In the days and weeks to come [of Fall 1995], you will read and hear a small army of eminent jurists, politicians and journalists responding with soothing assurances to popular outrage over the travesty of justice in the O.J. Simpson case. [In October 1995, a jury found Simpson not guilty of murdering his ex-wife and her friend.] They will tell you that, though fallible individuals sometimes make mistakes, the contemporary American jury system remains the best arrangement ever devised for ascertaining guilt and innocence. The jury system works.

Don't believe a word of it. The American jury system does not work to free the innocent and punish the guilty in an efficient and humane manner. It never has. Juries have always abused the institution, sacrificing impartial justice to political or ethnic goals. In Colonial America, the jury gave colonists a way to subvert local overlords appointed by London. From independence until the civil rights revolution, the jury was a means by which white bigots legally lynched Indians, blacks and Asians (or acquitted their white murderers). Today urban black juries all too often put race above justice in the same manner.

Even in a society less racially polarized than ours, the Anglo-American jury system would be a bad idea. The progress of civilization can be measured by the distance between the idea of crime as a matter between the criminal and his victim's relatives, and the idea of crime as an offense against the impersonal, constitutional state. The twelve-person jury, which the Vikings bequeathed to Anglo-Saxon England, lies on the barbaric end of the spectrum. For all the refinements of the past millennium, the jury system bears the marks of its primitive origins. There's the magical number twelve (about which irrational debates occasionally erupt when the idea of ten- or eleven-member panels is suggested). And there's the competition between attorneys and the ritual of cross-examination, which resemble, respectively, trial by combat and torture (both of which, come to think of it, were also jurisprudential approaches of the ancient Teutons).

Civil-Law Justice

Though the news may come as a surprise, juries as we know them are limited to the English-speaking, common-law world. Most other Western democracies have inherited their system of criminal justice from the continental European civil-law (Roman law) tradition. The contemporary civil-law tradition is not, as Anglo-American propaganda would have it, one of authoritarian, "inquisitorial" justice, with all-powerful judges railroading helpless innocents. On the contrary, all civil-law democracies today provide for some form of trial by jury. In civil-law countries, however, the jury is typically made up of a small number of professional and lay judges. The professional judges bring their experience to bear in sifting the evidence; the lay judges prevent the professionals from acting on the basis of prejudice or politics. Yet another professional judge presides over the trial (in some countries, impartiality is further assured by three-judge tribunals).

Reforming the Criminal Jury System

We need to have professional jurors, people with training in the law, who acquire enough experience not to be taken in by lawyers' tricks or appeals to their emotions. The identity of these jurors should be protected as tightly as the government conceals the identities of mobsters who have squealed on mafia kingpins. Protecting the integrity of the criminal justice system is at least as important as putting some mob leader behind bars.

One-way glass in front of the jury box would further secure their privacy and reduce the time-consuming theatrics of lawyers trying to appeal to the jurors' prejudices. When you don't know what color the jurors are, racial demagoguery becomes a much more risky tactic. When the lawyers can't read the jury's reactions to their antics in general, it makes playing it straight a much safer strategy.

Thomas Sowell, *Conservative Chronicle*, October 18, 1995.

The differences between the common-law and the civil-law approaches to criminal justice do not end with the composition of the jury. Grotesque battles over the admissibility of evidence like the Mark Fuhrman tapes just do not occur in the civil-law world, where the trial is usually preceded by a relatively calm investigation and examination under the direction of the public prosecutor and an examining judge. The defendant is treated more fairly, in these early phases, than in the United States. According to Stanford law professor John Henry Merryman in his study *The Civil Law Tradition*, "The dossier compiled by the examining magistrate is open to inspection by the defense, routinely providing information about the prosecution's case that in an American proceeding would be unavailable to the defense until its production was compelled by a motion for discovery or it was revealed at the trial." No surprise witnesses, no sealed evidence envelopes, no sleazy tricks during discovery.

Suppose that the United States, like France and Germany, had adopted its own national version of the civil-law system in the eighteenth or nineteenth century, in place of the British common-law inheritance—an American Civil Code, like the Code

Napoleon or the Prussian Code. Suppose, furthermore, that O.J. Simpson had been tried for murder under civil-law rules. How likely is it that the Simpson trial, in those circumstances, would have degenerated into an appalling spectacle of dirty tricks and bizarre legal hairsplitting? How likely is it that Johnnie Cochran would have played the race card and asked the jury to send a message to the L.A. police, if the jury had consisted of, say, Judge Ito and several other professional magistrates, as well as a few laymen? And the outcome of the Simpson case in a civil-law America? According to professor Merryman, "a statement made by an eminent comparative scholar after long and careful study is instructive: he said that if he were innocent, he would prefer to be tried by a civil-law court, but that if he were guilty, he would prefer to be tried by a common-law court."

An American Anachronism

I realize, of course, that by suggesting that we Americans might actually learn something from other countries I am questioning the dogma that the political and legal system of the United States has been perfect since its immaculate conception in an act of collective parthenogenesis by the Founding Fathers. The rules of American public discourse hold that no innovation in government or jurisprudence unknown to Americans before 1800, no matter how potentially beneficial, can be suggested for adoption; the opportunity for fundamental political and juridical thought in the U.S. came to an end with the close of the Founding era, rather as divine revelation is thought by Christians to have ceased at the close of the Apostolic Age.

While an intellectual tariff prevents the import of institutional improvements from abroad, Americans are free to export our superior system to the rest of the world. Indeed, doing so is something of a patriotic duty. Otherwise-educated Americans who happen to be completely unaware that our legal tradition is an eccentric deviation from the main tradition of Western jurisprudence do not hesitate to evangelize on behalf of the American Way in matters like criminal justice. In the first few years after the revolutions of 1989 in Europe, when post-communist states in Eastern Europe and Eurasia were debating different models of democratic constitutionalism (and usually concluding that the West German model is preferable to ours), a great number of representatives of the American bar flew into Eastern Europe to sing the praises of our malfunctioning separation-of-powers system and our even more disastrous jury system. My God, I remember thinking at the time, haven't the Eastern Europeans suffered enough?

We put up with an electoral system and a constitution in wigs and buckled shoes; why not tolerate a criminal justice system that wears a horned helmet and a bear skin? Here's why we should be concerned: the defects of our particular inherited structures of democratic and constitutional government may be mistakenly interpreted by an alienated public as failures of democracy and constitutionalism as such. The result of such unwarranted but understandable pessimism might be support for plebiscitary rule in politics and, perhaps, vigilantism in law enforcement. Huey Long will clean out the crooked statehouse; Charles Bronson or Clint Eastwood will punish the murderers who get off on technicalities. Legality cannot exist for long in the absence of legitimacy. In a contest between a law that seems to regularly produce unjust outcomes and extra-legal justice, rough justice in some form will sooner or later prevail. (How many people have *you* heard say, in response to news of Simpson's acquittal, "Maybe somebody will give him what he deserves?")

Junking Our Obsolete Heritage

To make the American system of criminal justice work will require intelligent reform, which in turn requires honest criticism and debate. Unfortunately, ever since Pearl Harbor, debate about fundamental institutional reform in this country has been deterred by the implication that critics of American political and legal institutions are traitors, with either "brown" or "red" sympathies. It is worth recalling that from the Civil War to Pearl Harbor we Americans progressed by junking large parts of the obsolete Anglo-American Colonial heritage and eclectically importing institutional innovations from abroad: the research university, the polytechnic and the kindergarten from Germany, the secret ballot from Australia, workmen's compensation from New Zealand, the public museum from France. As Japan has done recently, we shamelessly copied other nations and frequently improved on what we copied. During that era of American flexibility and progress, Oliver Wendell Holmes Jr., nobody's idea of a flaming radical, observed in connection with the common-law tradition that the mere fact that a statute goes back to the time of Henry VIII is not an argument in its favor.

In the spirit of the enlightened conservatism of Justice Holmes, we need to audit our inherited institutions, rescuing what is vital by carving away the deadwood. We can begin by admitting that some of the foreigners who look aghast at spectacles like the Simpson trial actually may have something to teach us about devising a criminal justice system capable of telling right from wrong.

"The jury system is a proven, effective, and important means of resolving civil disputes."

The Civil Jury System Is Effective

Civil Justice Reform Task Force

In June 1992, the Brookings Institution and the American Bar Association (ABA) Litigation Section cosponsored a symposium focusing on the civil jury system. The following viewpoint is excerpted from a report on the symposium that was issued by the Civil Justice Reform Task Force, a joint task force of the Brookings Institution and the ABA. The joint task force argues that although the jury system is not perfect, it is still an effective way of resolving civil conflicts. Juries are an important safeguard against judicial abuse of power, the task force contends. Furthermore, the task force asserts, juries serve the important function of balancing community values with legal justice. The Brookings Institution is an independent research organization that studies economics, government, foreign policy, and social sciences. The ABA Litigation Section is a professional organization for trial lawyers.

As you read, consider the following questions:

1. What reforms for the civil jury system are suggested by the joint task force?
2. According to the task force, what are the five virtues of the jury?
3. In what respect is the jury a great equalizer, according to the task force?

The right to a jury trial in civil cases is a fundamental feature of the American system of jurisprudence. It is enshrined in the Seventh Amendment to the Constitution and in similar provisions in most state constitutions.

In recent years, however, aspects of the civil justice system have been the subject of public discussion. At one level, debate has centered on substantive law and specifically on tort doctrines that allow injured individuals to recover compensation from those who have caused their injuries. At another level, discussions have focused on legal procedure and specifically the costs and delay in resolving civil disputes in the judicial system, as well as the quality of justice and the availability of the courts to the public at large. . . .

This viewpoint recounts an effort to move beyond these issues to consider the workings of the civil jury system itself, in both federal and state courts, throughout the country. The report that grows out of this effort represents a summary of the views of more than 100 individuals, many with in-depth knowledge of and broadly differing experiences with the civil jury system, all of whom met to discuss the future of that system at a symposium held in June 1992 in Charlottesville, Virginia. The participants included judges, academic researchers, communications specialists, law professors, attorneys specializing in representing plaintiffs and defendants, and representatives of users of the justice system—businesses, insurance companies, and public interest organizations. . . .

Our central conclusion is that the civil jury system is valuable and works well. Most of the participants do not believe it is "broken," and therefore it need not be "fixed." The jury system is a proven, effective, and important means of resolving civil disputes. Accordingly, there was strong sentiment among symposium participants to resist efforts to reduce the jury's role; indeed, some participants urged that the range of matters submitted for jury decisionmaking be expanded.

Improving the Jury System

At the same time, the symposium participants also generally recognized that, like all social institutions, the current jury system is not perfect. A challenge for the future is to enhance the effectiveness of the jury system.

In particular, an overwhelming proportion of the symposium participants agreed to the following proposals, which we describe as "strongly" supported:

• Jurors need not and should not be merely passive listeners in trials, but instead should be given the tools to become more active participants in the search for just results. To that end, trial procedures and evidentiary rules should take greater advantage of modern methods of communication and recognize modern understanding of how people learn and make decisions. Specifically, we strongly urge that jurors be allowed to take notes and that courts make more extensive use of visual exhibits (including videotapes and computer demonstrations).

• Judges can further enhance juror comprehension by providing preliminary instructions before trial and final instructions, tailored to the individual case, in clear, concise language free of legal jargon to the extent possible. In addition, copies of the instructions should be given to the jurors when they retire to deliberate.

• Much greater efforts should be made to improve conditions of jury service. Greater use should be made of the "one day–one trial" jury service practice now used in some courts. In addition, courts should schedule trials more flexibly for the convenience of jurors (including nights and weekends). Once a trial is in session, lawyers and judges should conduct the trial in a manner that would minimize juror inactivity. Juror compensation should be increased, and courts should regularly obtain feedback from jurors about their service. . . .

Virtues of the Jury

We affirm a strong commitment to a civil jury of lay persons. This is consistent with the strong support the public has given the jury system, as reflected in juror surveys, public opinion polls, the experience of trial judges and litigants, and the support of trial lawyers (regardless of whom they represent).

We provided many answers during the course of our deliberations to the question of what should be expected from the modern civil jury, both as decisionmaker in the small percentage of total cases that are tried and, perhaps more important, as a vehicle for influencing many cases that are settled or otherwise resolved in or out of the formal litigation system. The symposium participants believed that the jury fulfills both of those roles well.

More broadly, we identified five central virtues of the civil jury system, as compared with alternative means of resolving disputes.

First, the jury is a valuable process for decisionmaking and an effective means for arriving at a fair resolution of disputed facts. The evidence indicates the jurors take their responsibilities very seriously and attempt to reach fair and just results. Moreover, there is no evidence that judges or any other decisionmaker systematically would produce any more consistent or defensible set of results in similar circumstances than juries. Indeed, it is our collective experience, backed by the available empirical evidence, that the rate of agreement between judges and juries is generally high. As one participant observed, the amateurism and transience of the jury are its virtues, not its vices.

Second, the jury provides important protections against the abuse of power by legislatures, judges, the government, business, or other powerful entities. In the words of Chief Justice William Rehnquist, "the founders of our Nation considered the right to trial by jury in civil cases an important bulwark against tyranny and corruption, a safeguard too precious to be left to the whim of the sovereign, or, it might be added, to that of the judiciary." In principle, the jury system is a great equalizer, affording the opportunity for even the least powerful individuals in society to stand on equal footing with powerful interests once both are in a courtroom and where disputes are decided not by a single judge but instead by a randomly selected jury of individuals representative of a local community. Indeed, the protective role of the jury may become increasingly important as society becomes more complex, less connected, and more pluralistic.

A Superior Legal System

Are juries a main cause of problems in our legal system? To the contrary, they are one of the few things intrinsically right about American justice. Would our legal system be better off without juries? Hardly.

Judges are no better—and in several respects are much worse—at doing justice than juries.

Jurors collectively are as intelligent, fair and reasonable as any judge. They bring a collective common sense and a fresh, unjaded perspective to each individual case. Perhaps the jury system's greatest strength is that it combines the jurors' common sense with the judge's legal expertise. It is this ingenious mixture of checks, balances and complementary skills that makes our legal system superior to any that relies on judges alone.

Del Dickson, *San Diego Union-Tribune*, October 3, 1995.

Third, the jury brings broadly based community values to dispute resolution. Civil disputes are both private and public affairs. They are private in the sense that they arise only out of circumstances unique to the parties that bring them to the courts. But they are public because the standards used to resolve disputes on public standards are based on the community's sense of justice. Thus, the manner in which civil disputes are resolved also provides continued guidance to the rest of the society as to what is appropriate behavior.

We believe juries provide the best mechanism for bringing broadly based community values to bear on the issues involved in private disputes but doing so with their public function in mind. It is in the courtroom that the community's sense of fairness, of justice, of right and wrong is expressed. It is here that the conflict between the regulation of society and its impact on organizations and individuals gets adjusted and integrated, and where competing values are balanced.

The jury resolves concrete issues of "reasonableness," which legislatures often are unable to resolve in the face of scientific or other disputes. And it does so by bringing to the dispute resolution process the values not of one individual, such as a judge, but those of ordinary citizens who, in most cases, are more likely to be representative of the values of society as a whole. One of the discussion groups, for example, highlighted the fact that women and members of minority groups are far better represented in juries than they are among the judiciary. . . .

Fourth, the jury provides an important check on the bureaucratization and professionalization of the legal system. The involvement of jurors prevents adjudication from becoming technical and routinized, perhaps even distant and insensitive, as cases with similar fact patterns recur over and over before the same decisionmaker (the judge). The jury brings common sense and fairness to its decisions, cutting through the arcane and often overly detailed presentation of information by lawyers and judges. Lawyers can over-try cases, jury instructions can obfuscate basic legal principles, and judges can be mysterious and distant participants in the process. Juries tend, if the lawyers do not, to find the story that makes sense of the dispute and to base their judgments of fairness on the values and attitudes that jurors use in making their own decisions. So if lawyers, or judges, or the process fails to make it simple, the jury will.

Finally, the jury system provides a means for legitimizing the outcome of dispute resolution and facilitating public understanding and support for and confidence in our legal system. Law is the glue that helps hold society together. In a democratic society, confidence in the legal system is therefore essential. We believe citizens are more likely to have that confidence if the judicial system affords them a meaningful opportunity to participate than if they can be only bystanders or potential litigants. It is the possibility that anyone can serve on a jury that allows all of us to have confidence in the judicial system itself. Moreover, lay participation in adjudication through the jury system spreads knowledge of the law and the legal process throughout the nation. Jurors invariably report their respect for the jury system and their belief in its value.

"The Seventh Amendment in its guarantee of jury trials for civil cases involving twenty dollars or more is undesirable and should be withdrawn."

The Civil Jury System Should Be Abolished

Chester James Antieau

The Seventh Amendment to the U.S. Constitution guarantees the public the right to request a jury trial in civil cases that involve twenty dollars or more. In the following viewpoint Chester James Antieau argues that the amendment is outdated and should be abolished altogether. Using juries in civil cases prolongs trials and therefore makes them much more expensive than necessary, Antieau maintains. Many jurors are not competent enough to understand the issues in complex cases or their legal instructions, he contends, and they frequently disregard established laws in their decisions. Antieau is the author of *A U.S. Constitution for the Year 2000*, from which this viewpoint is taken.

As you read, consider the following questions:

1. What are the five reasons Antieau gives to support his contention that civil trial juries should be abolished?
2. On what factors do juries tend to base their decisions, according to the author?
3. Why is it preferable for a judge to decide a case rather than a jury, in Antieau's opinion?

Excerpted from *A U.S. Constitution for the Year 2000* by Chester James Antieau (Chicago: Loyola University Press, 1995). Reprinted by permission of the publisher.

The Seventh Amendment in its guarantee of jury trials for civil cases involving twenty dollars or more is undesirable and should be withdrawn by amendment.

First, from the language of the amendment and the intent of the people who framed and adopted it, it has always been understood that it does not require a civil jury in equity cases. Equity cases, it should be noted, have long involved fact issues as complex as law cases, and they have been resolved by judges sitting alone, to the satisfaction of the U.S. community. Likewise, it is firmly settled that persons litigating matters in admiralty, bankruptcy, military, and probate courts are not entitled to jury trials under the Seventh Amendment.

Second, it has been clearly established that the amendment does not require jury trials in civil actions created by Congress in which that body, explicitly or implicitly, indicates that adjudication of issues arising under the statute are to be determined in other ways. The United States Supreme Court ruled in 1977: "When Congress creates new statutory 'public rights,' it may assign their adjudication to an administrative agency with which a jury trial would be incompatible, without violating the Seventh Amendment injunction that jury trial is to be 'preserved' in suits at common law."

Third, it was understood at the time the Seventh Amendment was adopted that litigation of "summary" civil matters did not demand jury trials, and this has generally been accepted as another limitation upon the right to civil juries under the amendment. Illustratively, the United States Supreme Court has held that by the Constitution "a jury trial is not required in civil contempt proceedings." So, too, it has been held by that Court that trial by jury was not necessary in a disbarment action against an attorney. It has generally been held in the United States that in paternity proceedings, even where support for a child is asked, there is no constitutional right to jury trial. Jury trials are customarily denied in election contests, as well as in summary proceedings for the destruction of articles, such as gambling devices, held contra to law.

Delaying Justice

Fourth, the execution of justice is seriously delayed by using jury trials in civil cases. Initially the delay beings with the inordinate length of time needed to seat a jury, nineteen days in one reported case. Judges everywhere have complained of delays in administering justice caused by civil juries. Chief Judge Edward Devitt of the United States District Court for Minnesota is typical. He states: "It is fair to say that the backlog of cases in the federal courts, particularly in the metropolitan centers, is caused largely by the number of civil jury trials required by the Seventh

Amendment." New York Chief Justice Charles Desmond joined in criticizing the delays in New York courts caused by using juries in civil cases. David Peck, the presiding justice of the Appellate Division of the First Department of the New York Supreme Court, adds: "The inherent slowness of the process of jury trials is the root of delay wherever delay exists." He explained: "The average jury trial takes . . . three times as long as a trial before a judge without a jury." Another New York jurist, Joseph Proskauer, particularly lamented "the waste of time consumed in reading to a jury hour after hour and day after day written evidence which can be handed up to a trial judge and absorbed by him in a few minutes." To this must be added the hours spent by lawyers in extensive questioning of witnesses to make a point to jurors, the lengthy instructions by judges to clarify the issues of fact for the jurors, as well as time spent because of hung juries and subsequent retrials. A 1959 study by Harry Kalven, Hans Zeisel, and Bernard Bucholz concluded that jury trials took 67 percent more time than trials by the court, and they characterized as one of the "major defects" in our system of adjudicating legal issues "the extent to which trial by jury delays the disposition of cases."

Scrap the Jury System

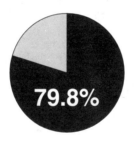

Of the more than 1300 readers who responded to *Parade*'s informal opinion survey, nearly four out of five (79.8%) would like to scrap the jury system entirely.

(A small number of them would replace it with professional jurors instead of judges.)

Marilyn vos Savant, *Parade*, July 30, 1995.

Fifth, experienced judges and capable scholars have seen the jury in civil cases as a very inefficient participant in the administration of justice. The competence of jurors to ascertain facts and apply the law to the facts has been seriously questioned. "Morality," rather than the law, has been seen as the basis for their verdicts. They have been said to be influenced by sentiment, and it has been written that their objectivity is "notoriously absent." Reportedly, they have arrived at verdicts by the flip of a coin, and an experienced trial lawyer, Joseph Welch, observed that juries are, out of sympathy, inclined to favor the younger lawyers. Altogether, concluded legal author Jerome Frank, they are "hopelessly incompetent fact-finders."

Juries and Complex Litigation

The inadequacy of the jury as trier of facts is especially acute in complex civil litigation. As early as 1927, a Canadian trial lawyer wrote: "Life has become too complex for the jury system. . . . The ascertainment of truth is a specialty, and it should now be assigned to men who by training and experience have qualified thereby for the duty." Since then litigation has become increasingly technical and complex, and it has been held that justice cannot be done by allowing civil trial juries to wade through entangled facts. Lord Patrick Devlin has persuasively made the case that in 1791, when the Seventh Amendment became effective, the Chancellor of England could take very complicated issues from law and assign them to chancery [a division of the British High Court of Justice that has jurisdiction over equity cases]. In other countries sharing our traditions it is possible for a judge to strike a request for a civil jury when he concludes, as in Ontario, that "the case is too complicated for a jury, or if the jury is likely to have difficulty remaining objective." Justice Walter Schaefer of the Illinois Supreme Court reports that doctors generally believe "their cases involve technical questions which are beyond the competence of a lay jury," and he then adds: "This feeling has considerable basis."

There is substantial basis for the belief that many jurors do not understand judges' instructions. Charles McCarter, an assistant attorney general for Kansas, questioned a hundred jurors, of whom twenty admitted they had not understood the instructions. Jerome Frank had earlier come to the same conclusion. After a 1947 Oklahoma study, John Hervey reported that as many as 39.5 percent of the jurors did not understand instructions.

Even when jurors understand instructions, there is evidence that they frequently disregard instructions on the law and refuse to apply the applicable law. One can suspect that they not only disregard the established law stated by judges, but that jurors make what they believe should be the law govern cases. It is reported that the United States Court of Appeals for the Tenth Circuit submitted a questionnaire to jurors, and their answers rather conclusively showed they had in effect repealed

34

the doctrine of contributory negligence and substituted that of comparative negligence. There is wide belief in the common law world that juries are governed by information or belief of things not properly before them under the applicable rules of evidence. Sir Patrick Devlin writes: "The fact that juries pay regard to considerations which the law requires them to ignore is generally accepted." Because so many of the rules of evidence have been imposed to prevent the jurors' being misled in their search for facts, abolishing juries in civil trials will greatly facilitate the introduction of germane evidence.

More Reasons for Abolishing Civil Juries

When issues are tried not by juries but by courts, the judges are customarily compelled to state their reasons for their findings and conclusions. This is of considerable aid to counsel in determining the advisability of an appeal, and of great value to appellate courts in deciding whether to sustain or reverse the action below. If a trial judge misconceives the facts, an appellate court can readily correct this and enter a proper judgment, whereas, if the facts were obviously misunderstood by jurors, appellate courts have only a very limited power to enter a corrected judgment.

Too much of the U.S. community's financial commitment to the administration of justice is dissipated on civil jury trials, which are exponentially more costly than trials before a court. Justice Henry Lummus of the Massachusetts Superior Court properly complains that "jury trials are always expensive for the public." Law professors Charles Clark and Harry Schulman conclude that "the protest against the expense of jury trials finds ample support in the facts."

Although it has been widely assumed that the Seventh Amendment requirement of trial by jury in civil cases involving twenty dollars is not binding upon the states, it remains possible that five members on the U.S. Supreme Court might hold this amendment applicable to the states and violated if a state chose to try all civil cases without a jury. The result would he horrendous, because in our federal system the states fully deserve the opportunity of experimenting not only with civil juries of members numbering fewer than twelve, but in totally abolishing juries in civil cases.

Trial juries in civil cases are not considered necessary to the execution of justice by the peoples of most of the world. Justice David Peck accurately reports that "Ours is the only country in the world which any longer attempts to handle civil litigation within the jury framework." Illustratively, in Germany and France, facts in civil cases are ascertained by judicial officers. Even in England, where the jury, as we know it, began, it is only in the most exceptional instance today that a civil trial jury is used. Civil juries have been almost completely abolished in countries that were part of the United Kingdom. Thus, in Australia the use of juries in civil litigation has virtually died a natural death. In Canada, juries are not generally used in civil cases. An exception remains in Ontario; however, even there, trial judges can in certain instances deny requests for juries. All but two of the sixteen Indian states have eliminated civil jury trials. In the United States, civil juries are seldom utilized in Louisiana.

A Scourge of U.S. Courts

In all frankness, our legal system makes us the laughingstock of the civilized world. France, Germany and many other European countries have an entirely different legal system that only occasionally uses juries—made up of select, qualified people. Japan and India attempted trial by jury and threw it out. Israel never even tried it. . . .

In *The Jury: Trial and Error in the American Courtroom*, Stephen Adler, legal editor of the *Wall Street Journal*, grimly predicts that a jury system that works as badly as ours "shouldn't, and won't, survive." He reconstructs the way jurors behaved in six conspicuous trials—one of which, in his judgment, was decided fairly, the other five ludicrously. He encountered lots of sincere, serious people who were "missing key points, focusing on irrelevant issues, failing to see through the cheapest appeals to sympathy or hate and generally botching the job."

Richard Grenier, *Insight*, December 12, 1994.

The people of the United States, virtually from our beginning as a nation, have seriously questioned the need to use juries in civil litigation. In *The Federalist Papers*, Alexander Hamilton wrote: "I cannot readily discern the inseparable connection between the existence of liberty, and the trial by jury in civil cases." In 1872, Mark Twain, who possessed a particular talent for sensing the views of the people, wrote: "The jury system puts a ban upon intelligence and honesty, and a premium upon ignorance, stupidity and perjury. It is a shame that we must continue to use a worthless system because it was good a thousand years ago." U.S. jurists have long acknowledged that trial juries are not necessary for the execution of justice in civil litigation. New York Justice Joseph Proskauer said in 1928: "The system of jury trial in civil contract cases has been transfixed from a useful process into a wasteful, ineffective and outworn fetish." He concluded: "There is no more practical reason today

36

for persisting in jury trial in this type of case than there would be for the continuance of trial by battle. . . .

Judges Versus Juries

Some segments of our society might suspect that they will be disadvantaged by judge trial rather than jury trial, but Justice David Peck has accumulated data from both New York and Los Angeles that clearly indicate that "the results obtained, or likely to be obtained from a jury trial or a non-jury trial are the same, both as to percentage of plaintiff and defendant verdicts, as well as to the amount received." The notion of the public in the United States that a jury trial is necessary in civil litigation for the attainment of justice, may well have been overestimated. Potential litigants have expressed their desires not to have juries hear their technical and/or complex cases. New York Justice Sydney Foster writes: "The bench and bar might get a rude shock at the dim view a great many laymen take as to jury trials in civil cases." He adds the further relevant factor: "Jury service is a hardship for many and an inconvenience, for most men at least."

The time is ripe to withdraw from the federal Constitution the requirement that juries must be made available upon request in civil court cases where twenty dollars or more are involved. . . .

Professor Kevin Kennedy has drafted a proposed constitutional amendment in these terms:

Section One: The Seventh Article of Amendment to the Constitution of the United States is hereby repealed.

Section Two: Except as otherwise provided by Congress, in civil actions brought in any court of the United States, all questions of fact shall be tried by a judge.

While this does not eliminate juries in all federal civil cases, it is a major move in the right direction and should be proposed by the Congress.

"Jurors have a right to protection . . . because press access to them risks compromising the core of their public roles."

Jury Deliberations Should Remain Secret

Abraham S. Goldstein

Traditionally, jury deliberations have been kept secret during and after a trial so that jurors may talk freely among themselves while reaching a decision. In the following viewpoint, Abraham S. Goldstein argues that the deliberation process is threatened by the increasing number of jurors who grant postverdict interviews with the media and write books about their experiences. If jurors know that their comments could be repeated outside the jury room and made subject to public scrutiny, they may feel constrained in their discussion of the case, Goldstein asserts. Therefore, he contends, all deliberations should be confidential except when jurors are allowed by the court to talk or write about their experiences. Goldstein is the Sterling Professor of Law at Yale Law School in New Haven, Connecticut.

As you read, consider the following questions:

1. What will be the result if jurors continue to give postverdict interviews to the media, in Goldstein's opinion?
2. What two methods does the author advocate for restricting the media's access to jurors?
3. Why is it unfair to jurors to ask them to explain their verdicts to the media, in Goldstein's opinion?

Excerpted from "Jury Secrecy and the Media: The Problem of Postverdict Interviews" by Abraham S. Goldstein, *University of Illinois Law Review*, vol. 1993, no. 2. Reprinted by permission.

For most of the petit jury's long history, and certainly since the nineteenth century, the secrecy of jury deliberations has been taken for granted. Like the outcome in trial by ordeal or trial by combat, the jury verdict has been regarded as divinely inspired. Prying into the jury's verdict, said William Holdsworth, would have been as "impious" as questioning the judgments of God. Today, the reasons for guarding secrecy are more functional than religious. It is now assumed that jurors must deliberate in secret so that they may communicate freely with one another, secure in the knowledge that what they say will not be passed along to others. As Justice Benjamin N. Cardozo wrote: "Freedom of debate might be stifled and independence of thought checked if jurors were made to feel that their arguments and ballots were to be freely published to the world." Moreover, secrecy is said to facilitate arriving at a group decision, bringing, according to John H. Wigmore, "community values" and common sense to bear on the decision, and sometimes dispensing with the law. Public confidence is even said to be enhanced by a verdict that is "difficult to disagree with because the secrecy of the jurors' deliberations and the general nature of the verdict make it hard to know precisely on what it was based," maintains Charles Nesson.

The Postverdict Inquisition

These policies are seriously threatened by interviewing jurors after a trial. In recent years, the seriousness of this threat has grown by several magnitudes. Newspapers and radio programs have quoted jurors extensively, jurors have appeared singly or in groups on television, and some have written articles and even books about their experiences. Reporters have telephoned jurors at home to arrange postverdict interviews. Hung juries have been questioned on the reasons for their inability to reach a verdict. Even sequestered jurors have been pursued by the media and have had questions shouted at them.

Popular culture is now grossly at odds with the jury's history and function. Potential jurors are being taught that their deliberations will not be secret at all. They can expect to be interviewed. They will be asked for their reasons and those of their fellow jurors for convicting, acquitting, or being unable to agree. And when they return an unpopular verdict, the postverdict "inquisition" by the media can easily take on the quality of attaint at common law, figuratively punishing jurors for doing their duty.

All this seems to have been happening in good faith, accompanied perhaps by a tinge of self-righteousness. To the media, the jury appears to be just another institution about which the public has a "right to know." As with "sunshine laws" [open meeting laws] and freedom of information acts, the operative assumption seems to be that the more we are told about how our institutions work, the more likely we are to have confidence in those institutions—or to learn they do not deserve our confidence and need correction. At the same time, if the media continue to reveal the contents of jury deliberations, there is a genuine risk that the authority of jury verdicts will decline—and that the jury will be less able to perform its distinctive constitutional role of restraining an arbitrary government. . . .

A Jury's Right to Privacy

The media claim a right of access to jury deliberations unless there is a compelling state interest in keeping them secret. Conceding that such an interest exists before the verdict, they argue that they must have reasonable access to jurors afterwards. They base this right of access on the "watchdog" role they play in learning about any and all information relevant to persons participating in a democratic society. Yet obviously there are limits. In the case of the jury, for example, jurors have rights of privacy and a wide range of critically important doctrines and practices depend upon the secrecy of the jury's deliberations. There is every reason to suppose that interrogation of jurors by the media is even more likely than questioning by lawyers and judges to interfere with the policies supporting privacy and secrecy. Simply put, journalists are not constrained in what they ask, as are lawyers, by professional discipline or by rules of ethics. Moreover, the defendant's right to a fair trial—by a jury confident that its deliberations will remain secret—is seriously threatened when jurors expect that they will have to face the media, or that their fellow jurors will talk to the media.

Persons asked to serve as jurors have a right to protection, not only in their private interest but in the larger social interest, because press access to them risks compromising the core of their public roles. Such access can and should be restricted. This might be done in several ways: by a court exercising its inherent authority over the jurors and the conduct of the trial (via general court rule or case-by-case) or by legislative enactment. The former probably would be easier to accomplish, at least until the media mobilized against it, and it would have the virtue of permitting experimentation at the local level. But statutes, state or federal, would be more likely to withstand constitutional challenge because they could affirm more clearly a compelling state interest in protecting the jury's deliberative processes—based upon legislative hearings demonstrating the effect of media interviews on potential jurors. The substance of such a statute would bar jurors from disclosing their deliberations and would bar anyone else (including the media) from seeking such disclosures without court permission. In the federal system, a statutory cousin to such a secrecy-guarding criminal provision already prohibits "recording, listening to, or observing proceedings of grand or petit juries while deliberating or voting." Additionally, in many jurisdictions efforts of the media to learn about secret grand jury proceedings have long been punishable by contempt. . . .

Restricting Publication of Deliberations

If a statute of the described sort were enacted, could the media publish truthful excerpts of deliberations obtained from jurors or others? The U.S. Supreme Court's opinion in *Florida Star v. B.J.F.* makes it clear that publication of truthful information is protected by the First Amendment only if it was lawfully obtained. If material is obtained unlawfully by the press, as from a juror known to be violating his statutory obligation, it would seem that the press may be punished and the publication may be restrained.

No Public Explanations

Many judges around the country are growing uncomfortable with the news media's focus on post-verdict interviews.

The main concern of some judges is that jurors even in mundane trials will be influenced by the highly visible roles they see "celebrity" jurors take. The judges fear that jurors won't feel safe speaking confidentially inside the jury room and will be less candid in their discussions.

"A great deal of attention is placed on jurors after they reach their verdict," said Judge Patricia J. Gifford, the Indianapolis state-court judge who presided over the Michael Tyson rape trial. "If jurors are learning that this [media attention] normally does happen, it would seem likely to influence them. A juror would think, 'If I vote this way, I'll have to explain why.'"

Judges and others alarmed about post-verdict interviews say that revealing the workings of jury deliberations—which tend to be more art than science—could weaken public confidence in verdicts. Juries don't necessarily reason the way a judge or lawyer would, and they often make compromises the law doesn't specifically allow.

Wade Lambert, *Wall Street Journal*, December 30, 1993.

Should (and can) such a statute bar the media from publishing deliberation material that comes to them without their knowing participation—e.g. "over the transom"? Such material may come from unknown sources or already may be in circulation by virtue of improper disclosures by jurors, attorneys, or others.

Yet its publication obviously will affect how potential jurors regard the secrecy of their deliberations. In the *Pentagon Papers Case* [*New York Times Co. v. United States*], Justice Byron White distinguished between imposing criminal sanctions for actual publication of statutorily protected material and restraining the publication in advance, implicitly suggesting that the former would be permissible but the latter would not, unless it could meet the heavy burden placed upon a "prior restraint." Such restraint can be justified only by showing it is necessary to prevent a "clear and present danger" to the administration of justice. Making such a showing would be extraordinarily difficult. Circumstances may arise, however, that might demonstrate the need for prior restraint for a limited period. For example, in the much-publicized case involving the police beating of Rodney King, there was a hung jury and a decision to retry one of the charges. Given the expectable difficulty of finding a new jury that was unfamiliar with the case, and the further difficulty of finding jurors unafraid to serve in the second trial, it should have been permissible for the trial judge, at the close of the first case, to direct the media not to publish any accounts of the first jury's deliberations, even if innocently acquired—at least until after the second jury had been selected.

Keep Deliberations Confidential

The court should tell jurors that what they say to each other is said in confidence and that if they breach the confidence they can be subjected to sanctions. The media, too, should be put on notice that interviewing jurors about their deliberations without first obtaining court permission is an unlawful solicitation or attempt to breach the confidence and that publication of disclosures about jury deliberations, knowingly in violation of such a court rule or statute, is punishable.

An effort to restrict postverdict interviewing surely will lead to questions about whether it is really important to keep the media from piercing, to a limited degree, the secrecy of the jury room—particularly because systematic research has not been conducted to determine whether individuals and groups are affected by knowledge that their behavior subsequently may be exposed. It will be asked how we can know whether jurors and their deliberations deserve public confidence unless we allow the press to interview jurors—whether newly visible jurors will be courageous rather than craven, rational rather than irrational. Besides, if we let the media interview jurors, it does not follow that they will do so in all cases or that jurors will answer. It could then be said that occasional interviews and even more occasional publication of those interviews would be a window on the jury—a sample of its work to help the public determine whether the institution is performing its assigned role.

Some also have suggested that it is long past time to demystify the jury. In this view, jurors are public servants; exposing them to public scrutiny would enhance their accountability to the community they represent. Besides, much of the received wisdom about secrecy may not bear close scrutiny. Though intuitively compelling, it depends upon the assumption that jurors will not perform their distinctive historic role if they could no longer expect that their deliberations would remain secret. Yet that assumption may be incorrect. At present, jurors' votes for conviction or acquittal, which are the ultimate tests of whether they are willing to take a stand against arbitrary government, obviously will be known (at least where a unanimous verdict is required). It is not at all clear why the fact that their conversations in the jury room also may come to be known will make them less courageous. Moreover, jurors may become accustomed to the presence of the media. This may make them *more* independent, at least in some cases, rather than less so. For example, they may be fearful that views favoring conviction might become known in "mob" cases but not at all fearful of challenging the actions of the prosecutor and judge.

Letting the Genie Out of the Bottle

In the end, these are the grosses of speculations. If we let the genie out of the bottle, we probably will be unable to put it back again. The media seek interviews in the most sensational cases, in which public attention is highest. Jurors called to serve in such cases will expect to be interviewed and will expect their fellow jurors to be interviewed. Inevitably, that expectation will affect how freely they talk to each other; it will make them feel visible to the world and accountable as individuals, not as a body. The previously anonymous jurors, reaching a group decision based on "community values" and lay perspectives, will feel they must justify it in the court of public opinion.

We will then be asking of jurors that they be like judges— heroic and principled and standing up for their decisions in written findings and decisions. Yet we do not give jurors the robes, the tenure, the professional training, and the perquisites to make it either fair or appropriate to ask them to play so public a role. Unchecked, the interviewing of jurors in high visibility cases will expose to view "the difficult and uniquely human judgments that defy codification and that 'build discretion, equity and flexibility into a legal system'" [the U.S. Supreme Court in *McClesky v. Kemp*, quoting from Harry Kalven and Hans Zeisel's book *The American Jury*]. That, in turn, surely will unravel the distinctive nonrational and intuitive "genius" of this lay tribunal.

We do not write on a blank slate. We are constrained greatly in changing the jury because its several functions are so interconnected and so integrally related to historic doctrines, practices, and institutions. We proceed at our peril, therefore, both constitutionally and functionally, when we challenge one of the jury's core characteristics. The inscrutability of the jury verdict, and the secrecy through which it is maintained, writes William R. Cornish, "is surely [such] a characteristic . . . [and] is bound to last as long as the jury system itself. Once the inscrutability principle has gone, the time has come to set up another kind of tribunal." If we assume, as I do, that there is a great deal to question about the prevailing system of jury trial, it does not follow that answers to those questions should be forced on us as unanticipated consequences of allowing the media to have access to jury deliberations. Nor does it follow that we will learn best from unbridled interviews about how jurors function. If we would pursue that objective, either for research or for law reform purposes, we would be better served by requiring court authorization for such interviews in particular cases.

"Juror speech . . . is valuable expression that teaches us about the functioning of one of our most important institutions, and ensures openness and fairness in the process."

Revealing Jury Deliberations Can Help the Judicial Process

Marcy Strauss

Marcy Strauss is a law professor at Loyola Law School in Los Angeles. In the following viewpoint, Strauss argues that juror journalism—the practice of jurors' selling their stories to the media after a trial—has been unfairly criticized as harmful to the judicial process. She maintains that no studies have shown that juror journalism actually has had an adverse effect on jury deliberations. In fact, Strauss contends, juror journalism may help lawyers, judges, and the public understand trials, juries, and their deliberations better by exposing flaws in or abuses of the judicial system.

As you read, consider the following questions:

1. How could a juror's plans to write about the deliberations affect other members of the jury, according to Strauss?
2. Why is the First Amendment's protection of juror speech important, in the author's view?
3. According to Strauss, in what ways can juror journalism reveal positive aspects of the judicial process?

Excerpted from "Juror Journalism" by Marcy Strauss. Reprinted by permission of The Yale Law Journal Company and Fred B. Rothman & Co. from the *Yale Law & Policy Review*, vol. 12, no. 2 (1994), pp. 389–423.

The conflict between freedom of speech and the right to a fair trial is hardly new. Hundreds of articles have been written attempting to reconcile the constitutional demand that the defendant receives a fair trial with First Amendment issues posed by pretrial publicity, cameras in the courtroom, or the gagging of lawyers who attempt to try their cases in public. In recent years, however, a new face to the conflict has appeared, having to do not with lawyers or the news media, but with the jury. Increasingly, individuals have tried to capitalize on their jury service by selling their perspective on the trial. This practice of "juror journalism" has been criticized by numerous academics and even lambasted by many journalists as threatening the integrity and fairness of the trial. The fear is that the profit motive may affect the juror's ability to fairly, openly, and without bias deliberate and render a just verdict.

In response to this fear, numerous cities and states have begun to consider statutes regulating or prohibiting juror journalism; several states have adopted laws restricting jurors' ability to contract for profit during the pendency of the trial. The incredible amount of checkbook journalism which occurred during the pretrial phase of the O.J. Simpson trial prompted Superior Court Judge Lance Ito to adopt measures that went beyond any existing statutory provision in restricting jurors' speech. In a court order dated September 23, 1994, he declared that every juror and alternate juror had to agree "not to request, accept, agree to accept, or discuss with any person receiving or accepting, any payment or benefit in consideration for supplying any information concerning this trial *for a period of 180 days* from the return of a verdict or the termination of the case, whichever is earlier." Such statutes and judicial orders raise an important question: Can juror speech be silenced or even restricted consistent with the First Amendment's guarantee of freedom of expression and freedom of the press? . . .

The Extent of Juror Journalism

The idea of juror as profiteer has so flourished in recent years that Kenneth Jost felt compelled to label this era the "dawn of . . . big-bucks juror journalism." This phenomenon, moreover, is likely to escalate further as trials become more highly publicized. Televised proceedings like those involving William Kennedy Smith [acquitted of rape in Palm Beach, Florida, in 1991], Rodney King [the black motorist who was forcefully subdued by four white Los Angeles police officers in 1991], Amy Fisher [the teenager who shot the wife of her lover, Joey Buttafuoco, in 1992], the Menendez brothers [who were tried for the 1989 murder of their parents in 1993 and 1995 in Los Angeles] and, most recently and most significantly, O.J. Simpson whet the public's appetite for news, stories and even made-for-television movies about "real" courtroom dramas. The juror's perspective is one which will be increasingly sought. After all, the juror is not only an insider at the trial, but the decisionmaker as well. And, unlike the judge, the lawyers, or even the parties to the suit, the juror is someone with whom the public can easily identify. Consequently, the media and entertainment industry will increasingly approach jurors, and more and more jurors can be expected to seek out the spotlight. As one news reporter cynically remarked, "Who would have guessed it? The juror as superstar."

That jurors themselves anticipate potential royalties and aspire to write articles, bestsellers or even movie scripts is borne out by numerous examples. Perhaps the best known example of juror journalism arose out of the trial of Bernard Goetz, who was accused of shooting several youths who had attempted to mug him in a New York subway. When Mark Lesly was selected as a juror in the trial, he decided to dictate his daily impressions of the case into a tape recorder. He did so, Lesly said, because he wanted a record of the experience and because he "had a reasonable belief that it might be worth something."

He was right. Several days after the jury acquitted Goetz of all but a gun possession charge, Lesly sold a three-part account of the trial to the *New York Post* for close to $5,000. Another juror, Diane Serpe, was paid $2,500 by the *Daily News* for her "view from the jury box."

A Lucrative Responsibility

Lesly and Serpe are not the first, nor the last, according to Michael Freitag, to discover that "jury duty, usually regarded as a thankless civic responsibility, can be lucrative." Even several book deals have been negotiated. James Shannon, a juror in the Pennzoil-Texaco case, wrote a book on the trial after receiving an advance in the low five figures from Prentice-Hall. A juror in the General William Westmoreland libel suit against CBS received $15,000 for her book on the trial—"The Juror and the General"—published by William Morrow and Co. . . .

While the known number of juror journalists might appear small, these stories represent only the tip of the iceberg. For every juror who succeeds in profiteering from jury service, undoubtedly many contemplate such a prospect, and others likely try and fail. A precise count of such activity is impossible. The number of jurors contemplating fame and fortune, however, will almost certainly increase substantially in the future. The expanding practice of cameras in courtrooms, the public's voracious appetite for crime stories and real-life dramas, the proliferation of talk shows encouraging jurors to reveal the inside details about sensational trials—all these operate to ensure an ever-expanding number of persons seeking to use their jury experience for personal gain. . . .

Juror Journalism's Effect on Other Jurors

Juror journalism risks not only the integrity of the juror seeking profit; it may also impose on the other jurors as well. Most significantly, the knowledge (or even the belief) that a member of the jury is writing or planning to write about the trial may inhibit the frank and open exchange of ideas in deliberations. Simply, jurors may be reluctant to express minority or unpopular views if they believe that such opinions will be aired to the public. As Justice Benjamin N. Cardozo wrote, "[f]reedom of debate might be stifled and independence of thought checked if jurors were made to feel that their arguments and ballots were to be freely published to the world." This rationale for juror secrecy may not only apply to confidentiality during the deliberative process itself; if jurors believe that others will freely discuss the thoughts and deliberation of their colleagues after the verdict is returned, the free-flowing process that our system encourages may be chilled.

This frank and open exchange by jurors, moreover, is critical to the effectiveness of the decisionmaking process. Resolution by jury is valued precisely because of the deliberative nature of the process. A just consensus is most likely to be reached after an open exchange of ideas and beliefs on the credibility and motivation of witnesses and the fairness of various decisions. Without such dialogue, the wisdom and fairness of jury verdicts would be in doubt. The process could not be trusted.

Additionally, jurors, fearing exposure of their deliberations to the public, may be discouraged from reaching unpopular decisions. As one author noted:

> Jurors' willingness to depart from community expectations becomes even less probable if a wide audience may discover precisely how much each individual contributed to an unpopular verdict or which jurors delayed or thwarted a popular one. A juror who realizes . . . that deliberations may become a part of the public domain is less likely to argue for judgments contrary to public opinion and the deliberative process is therefore less likely to produce them.

While the impact of juror journalism on jury deliberations is potentially great, there are a number of considerations that at least challenge the significance of this problem. First, how often do other jurors fear such publicity? That is, even when a juror is writing or plans on writing about the trial, do the other jurors know about this? Or has juror journalism in sensational trials reached such a level that jurors presume or fear that information about the deliberations will be revealed? It should be remembered that the number of cases in which jurors contemplate writing a book or selling the story is, comparatively speaking, minuscule. While there are a few examples of juror journalists revealing their intentions to other jurors, the precise scope of this problem cannot be quantified. Thus, perhaps the worst that can be said is that while the magnitude of the harm may be great, the significance of the problem is unknown.

Checkbook Justice or Free Speech?

Distasteful as it is to some observers, jurors are free under the First Amendment to write books for profit about their jury experience. Some may fear that jurors will let the hope of profit influence their behavior. They might, for example, hold out against other jurors to heighten the drama and the commercial value of their own stories. But the Supreme Court held unanimously in 1991 that even a convicted criminal cannot be denied compensation for articles or books about the crime.

The worst fears about "checkbook journalism" must be balanced against the value of exposing what actually goes on in the jury room. Judges, lawyers and lay observers have often learned how well—or how poorly—the jurors understood the evidence or obeyed the judge's legal instructions.

The New York Times, June 4, 1995.

Second, even the magnitude of the harm may not be as significant as on first consideration. That is, even if jurors believe that the deliberations may be publicized, this may enhance, not detract from, the quality of the deliberations. The assumption that juror deliberations must be conducted in private concededly has been long accepted and rarely questioned. Perhaps it is appropriate now at least to question the need for secrecy at least within the context of jurors later recollecting the deliberation process rather than preventing people from eavesdropping on the actual deliberation. After all, in most other areas of government, the move to open up proceedings to the public stems from the belief that public scrutiny *benefits* the deliberative process. Similarly, it is possible to argue that a juror who knows or suspects that the jury deliberations may become public will be more conscientious, thoughtful, and challenging of others in order to ensure the most defensible verdict.

Study Shows No Difference

A study conducted with mock jurors seems to bear out this supposition. In the study, half the juries were told that their deliberations would be private, and half were told that the deliberations would be reviewed by a panel of psychologists and legal experts and that they might be invited to discuss the argument and opinions they had expressed. Although John Davis and the other researchers ultimately found no difference in verdicts between the two groups, they concluded:

> [the] private-condition jurors may adopt an early opinion and feel less inclined to change with time. They perhaps feel less need than public condition jurors to debate, examine, and generally test testimony interpretations, recall, etc., since they do not expect subsequent challenge. Public condition jurors perhaps reacted to the expected scrutiny by playing the role of a particularly conscientious juror. They consequently attempted to avoid "premature" opinion change, and with repeated refutation and counterarguments felt increasingly free to alter their opinion.

Thus, the impact of juror journalism on the deliberative process remains uncertain. It has historically been assumed that the deliberation process must be conducted in secret in order to encourage frank and open discussion; whether this presumption applies only during the actual deliberation process itself, or whether it also applies to a fear of future revelation, has never been established. Yet despite the absence of proof, those lamenting juror journalism still continue to simply assert the importance of secrecy. This mere assertion, however, should not be sufficient to condemn juror journalism, particularly because there is at least some evidence that the possibility of future revelation has a desirable effect on jury deliberations. . . .

The Value of Juror Speech

Why not ban or restrict juror speech? I explore that question by considering the value of freedom of expression in the context of juror journalism. Should society care about protecting juror speech? Is it the kind of expression that should be valued under the First Amendment?

Juror speech fosters many important values in society—values recognized as compelling by the First Amendment. A core value of the First Amendment is ensuring speech that facilitates democracy and self-government. Because the people are sovereign, they must have access to information allowing them to evaluate governmental processes, including the court system. As the Supreme Court noted in 1991, "[t]he judicial system, and in particular our criminal justice courts, play a vital part in a democratic state and the public has a legitimate interest in their operations." As Michael E. Swartz stated, "the public has a right to know about the operations of the judicial branch, an agency of democratic government." Indeed, as was noted in *Richmond Newspapers Inc. v. Virginia,* "it would be difficult to single out any aspect of government of higher concern and importance to the people than the manner in which criminal trials are conducted. . . ."

Speech that explores, criticizes, or merely reveals information about the judiciary falls squarely within this protected area of speech. Juror speech, in other words, serves an essential function in a democracy by revealing flaws, inconsistencies, or unfairness in the judicial process. Juror speech may illuminate incompetence, inefficiency, and corruption in the court system. Moreover, the mere knowledge that jurors can speak freely about the trial and its participants may help to ensure a fair process. "The knowledge that every criminal trial is subject to contemporaneous review in the forum of public opinion is an effective restraint on possible abuse of judicial power. . . . Without publicity, all other checks are insufficient; in comparison of publicity, all other checks are of small account," as was pointed out in *In re* Oliver.

Besides exposing possible flaws in the system or deterring potential abuses, juror speech is also valuable even when revealing what is good about the system. Explanations of how the deliberations progressed could reinforce notions that the jury system does work and thus increase public confidence that justice was served. A juror's description of how a particular verdict was reached may help justify a verdict that appeared to the public to be grossly unfair, and therefore preserve the integrity of the judicial system generally and the role of the jury specifically. Consider, for example, the effect of the jurors speaking out after the acquittals of the four police officers accused in a state proceeding of using unreasonable force against Rodney King. Although many still disagreed with the verdict, the explanations at least may have assured some members of the public that the verdict was based on a certain interpretation of the evidence and could not simply be dismissed as the result of blatant racism.

An Aid to Understanding

Finally, juror speech aids lawyers, scholars, and laypersons in understanding the judicial process. As such, it plays an essential role in any attempt to better the justice system. Lawyers frequently request access to jurors after the verdict in order to learn more about their own shortcomings at trial. Scholars may question jurors to assess the effect of various legal tactics, to determine the juries' interpretation of judicial instructions, and to better understand the dynamics of the deliberation process. Jurors' discussion about their trial experience educates the public about their own duties and obligation of jury service. In sum, even when juror journalism is pedantic, it still serves an essential informational function about the justice system.

Besides facilitating democracy and self-government, juror

speech is valuable because it enhances the personal growth and self-fulfillment of the speaker. As was noted in *Bose Corporation v. Consumers Union*, "[T]he freedom to speak one's mind is . . . an aspect of individual liberty—and thus a good unto itself. . . ." In expressing our own thoughts and ideas, we grow as individuals; revealing our inner feelings can serve as a catharsis. Juror speech serves these objectives. As jury expert Hans Zeisel has noted, the urge to talk about the experience of jury duty is a strong one, in part to release the pent-up emotional pressure inherent in the role of juror. Especially when unpopular verdicts are reached, jurors often feel compelled to publicly defend themselves against charges of bias and incompetence. . . .

A Valuable Expression

There is no dispute that juror journalism is disquieting; it raises legitimate questions that require further exploration and study. Hopefully, this viewpoint will inspire such research, particularly attempts at empirical analysis to answer many of the questions raised within. For the time being, the lack of any real empirical evidence militates against any regulation of juror speech. Yet this lack of proof of harm has not stemmed the virulent attack by some on juror journalism; it has not stopped three states from prohibiting jurors from contracting to sell their story during the trial. In the rush to condemn jurors' attempts to profit, it is all too easy to ignore or minimize the First Amendment values implicated. Juror speech, be it motivated by profit or by more altruistic reasons, is valuable expression that teaches us about the functioning of one of our most important institutions, and ensures openness and fairness in the process. Given the current paucity of evidence concerning the real effects of juror profiting on a fair trial, government regulation that risks chilling juror speech is too high a price to pay.

Periodical Bibliography

The following articles have been selected to supplement the diverse views presented in this chapter. Addresses are provided for periodicals not indexed in the *Readers' Guide to Periodical Literature*, the *Alternative Press Index*, or the *Social Sciences Index*.

Stephen J. Adler	"Jury Trials and the Wizards of Odds," *American Enterprise*, November/December 1994.
Stephen J. Adler	"We the Jury Find . . . ," *Responsive Community*, Winter 1994/95. Available from 2020 Pennsylvania Ave. NW, Suite 282, Washington, DC 20006.
Christopher Baldwin	"Jury-Rigging," *Chronicles*, March 1995. Available from 934 N. Main St., Rockford, IL 61103-7061.
Barbara Bradley	"Juries and Justice: Is the System Obsolete?" *Insight*, April 24, 1995. Available from 3600 New York Ave. NE, Washington, DC 20002.
CQ Researcher	"The Jury System," November 10, 1995. Available from 1414 22nd St. NW, Washington, DC 20037.
George P. Fletcher	"Convicting the Victim," *New York Times*, February 7, 1994.
Sophfronia Scott Gregory	"Oprah! Oprah in the Court!" *Time*, June 6, 1994.
Barbara Holland	"Do You Swear That You Will Well and Truly Try . . . ?" *Smithsonian*, March 1995.
John Leo	"Watching 'As the Jury Turns,'" *U.S. News & World Report*, February 14, 1994.
Mark Miller	"Molding the Perfect Jury," *Newsweek*, August 22, 1994.
Richard A. Posner	"Juries on Trial," *Commentary*, March 1995.
Religion & Society Report	"The End of the Jury System," May 1994. Available from 934 N. Main St., Rockford, IL 61103-7061.
Chi Chi Sileo	"Fringe Groups and Militias Aim to 'Restore' Constitution," *Insight*, August 21, 1995.
David O. Stewart	"Uncertainty About Reasonable Doubt," *ABA Journal*, June 1994. Available from 750 N. Lake Shore Dr., Chicago, IL 60611.
Hiller B. Zobel	"The Jury on Trial," *American Heritage*, July/August 1995.

Does the Civil Justice System Need Reform?

The
Legal
System

Chapter Preface

Stella Liebeck, 79, was sitting in a parked car in an Albuquerque McDonald's parking lot with her son-in-law, Charles Allen, in 1992 when she accidentally spilled scalding coffee on herself and the car seat while trying to remove the cup's lid to add cream and sugar. The 180-degree coffee caused third-degree burns on her inner thighs, groin, and buttocks. Liebeck was in the hospital for eight days, received two skin grafts, and required two years to fully recover. Her hospital bills totaled more than $10,000. When she asked McDonald's to reimburse her for her medical costs, the fast food corporation offered her $800. She sued.

During the 1994 jury trial, McDonald's admitted it had received 700 reports of burns from its coffee, but considered them "statistically insignificant" in light of the fact that it sold one billion cups of coffee a year. Corporate policy decreed that the coffee temperature be between 180 degrees and 190 degrees—40 to 50 degrees hotter than the coffee at most other restaurants—because the hotter temperature made the coffee taste better.

The jury awarded Liebeck $200,000 in damages but deducted $40,000 because of her negligence. It then fined McDonald's $2.7 million for punitive damages, the equivalent of two days' worth of coffee sales. The judge reduced the punitive damages award to $480,000, or three times Liebeck's actual damages. Rather than appealing the case, McDonald's settled later with Liebeck for an undisclosed amount.

Inspired partially by the *Liebeck v. McDonald's* case and other high-profile jury awards, many in Congress have advocated reform of America's civil justice system. Proposed legislation includes a bill called "loser pays," which would require the losing party in a lawsuit to pay the winner's attorney's fees, and a bill that would cap punitive damages at three times the actual damages, or $250,000, whichever is greater. The authors of the following viewpoints debate whether these reforms are necessary.

"What flaws the current system is its sheer unpredictability and the arbitrary disbursement of justice that results."

The Civil Justice System Needs Reform

Liz Spayd

The current civil justice system is flawed by the arbitrariness of the justice meted out, argues Liz Spayd in the following viewpoint. Furthermore, the fear of legal liability and the escalating costs of lawsuits lead many companies to abandon the development of new products or remove them from the market, she maintains. Reforming the civil justice system by defining culpability and instituting a national standard for monetary damages would result in more equitable judgments, Spayd contends. Spayd is an editor for the *Washington Post* newspaper.

As you read, consider the following questions:

1. According to Spayd, how much does society spend each year on the tort system?
2. What reforms are needed to fix the civil justice system, in the author's opinion?
3. Why should the amount of punitive damages be limited, in Spayd's view?

Liz Spayd, "Taking the Ball Out of the Court," *Washington Post National Weekly Edition*, March 13–19, 1995; ©1995, Washington Post Writers Group. Reprinted with permission.

Suppose for a moment that a small drug company miraculously discovers a vaccine that can prevent cancer. And suppose that its new drug is cheap, easy to administer and has but a single, albeit serious, drawback: One in 10,000 people who take it may experience acute vision loss. Should the company bring the product to market, figuring that a relative handful of people may go blind so that millions of lives can be saved?

At most companies, this is not so much a moral dilemma as it is a legal one. Compelled by simple mathematics, the drug manufacturer's lawyers would almost certainly advise that the product be scrapped. Consider, after all, that one in nine people will be diagnosed with cancer, that millions of those who already have the disease or are at high risk of developing it would take the wonder drug and that hundreds of them could go blind. Even with government approval and the usual warnings about side-effects, the company—though not intending harm—could be accused of having acted negligently. With the drug-maker risking exposure to billions of dollars in damages, it would be economic suicide not to shelve the product completely.

How is it that we developed a civil justice system that rewards caution and punishes scientific innovation? That embraces the notion of consumer as victim and dismisses the concept of individual responsibility? That targets not just the pharmaceutical company with a potential cure for cancer but even the fast-food restaurant that brews its coffee too hot, the bartender who doesn't save the drunkard from his vice, the automaker that allows its windshield to shatter when the driver veers into a tree?

Over the past half century, the cost of personal-injury, product-liability and medical-malpractice cases—so-called torts—has grown at four times the rate of the overall economy to the point where society now doles out some $130 billion a year to pay the legal fees, the damage awards and general overhead required to sustain such a system. The number of tort cases in both federal and state courts has been climbing sharply, as has the number of lawyers anxious to settle these and other disputes arising from our increasingly litigious society. Since the 1970s, the number of lawyers in this country has doubled to more than 800,000.

Bad enough that we tie up so many resources on what is essentially an unproductive wedge of our economy. Worse that we have created a legal system that thrives on the false premise that every accident can be traced back to a callous wrongdoer.

A Uniform National Standard

This is not social progress. Nor is it easily fixed. Legal reforms being debated in the House in 1995 promise to be the most intensely lobbied and difficult-to-enact provisions of the Republican "Contract With America" [ten reforms proposed by the 1995

Republican-led Congress during its first 100 days]. Against the wishes of well-funded trial lawyers and vocal consumer groups, the legislation would place strict new limits on punitive damages and impose other changes that would bring relief to businesses facing costly litigation. By replacing a patchwork of state laws with a uniform national standard, the legislation would go a long way toward fixing a legal system that is now badly broken. [The Product Liability Fairness Act, H.R. 956, was passed by the House March 10, 1995, and by the Senate May 10, 1995.]

"AWK! REFORM TORT LAW?! AWK! BUT THAT WOULD PENALIZE THE LITTLE GUY!!"

Henry Payne reprinted by permission of United Feature Syndicate, Inc.

More than anything, what flaws the current system is its sheer unpredictability and the arbitrary disbursement of justice that results. In theory, by allowing people to file civil claims, corporate and individual miscreants can be punished while still leaving the police and prosecutors free to go after murderers, rapists and other violent offenders. But the way the system has evolved, the defendants in civil suits wind up facing judgment without a fraction of the rights afforded criminal suspects.

In most states, there is no limit to the amount of monetary damages a company could be required to pay, no clear definition of what constitutes a "crime" and no requirement that the plaintiff prove the company acted maliciously.

"Nowhere in the world do we have punishments without limits," complains Victor Schwartz, a Washington attorney who helped draft legal reform efforts for both the Ford and Carter administrations and is now working with the new Republican leadership.

Limiting Punitive Damages

The proposals before Congress would change that situation. Both the House Judiciary and Commerce committees have approved bills that would limit punitive damages to the greater of $250,000 or three times the plaintiff's economic damages from such things as lost income and medical expenses. The reforms would also more clearly define culpability: Punitive damages could be awarded only if there were clear and convincing evidence that the defendant flagrantly disregarded the safety of others. As it is now, in many states jurors need only determine that the chances were better than 50–50 that the defendant acted with gross negligence.

There are other strange notions of justice embedded in the current system. It is common wisdom that in a typical product-liability or personal-injury suit, the victim's lawyers look for three characteristics in the defendants they go after: someone to fault, someone to hate and someone to pay. And in most states, the plaintiff is allowed to sue anyone who might have played even a minor role in causing an accident or injury. Under this doctrine, if the company or person with primary responsibility doesn't have much money, you go after someone who does. And if there is an oil or chemical company with even tangential involvement, by all means target it—so notorious are juries for returning big judgments against this villainous lot.

Unequal Justice

The problem with this set-up is that justice isn't apportioned equitably. Gates Corp., a tire and rubber manufacturer in Denver, is now one of 45 defendants being blamed for the 1991 fire at a North Carolina chicken-processing plant that killed 25 people. Never mind that there was no fire alarm, no sprinkler system and no way for the workers to get out through the locked exit doors. Since the building owner is bankrupt, Gates is being sued because its rubber hoses, along with many other flammable products inside the plant, caught fire and allegedly contributed to the toxic fumes that engulfed the facility. Under the proposed legal reforms, a company would be responsible only for the proportion of the pain and suffering damages that resulted from its product.

As it is, Gates spends $3.5 million a year defending itself against such suits—because one of its fan belts is blamed for a car accident or because one of its power-steering hoses is cited as the reason someone lost control of their vehicle.

And as a practical matter, says Gates vice president Thomas J. Gibson, it isn't up to the plaintiff to prove that a faulty fan belt indeed caused the accident, but up to Gates to prove it didn't. Nor does the typical decision to fight or settle turn on whether the company considers itself guilty or not.

Nowadays, decisions like these are driven less by morality than by economics.

"Somewhere along the way, you have to ask yourself, 'Why don't we just pay the $100,000 to settle the thing instead of spending five times that defending ourselves?'" Gibson says. "It's extortion, but we've had cases where we've felt that's the better way to go . . . and I cringe when I sign the checks."

Even worse, Gibson says, those who cave in are feeding the very system they despise. If there are a dozen defendants in a personal injury suit, for example, the settlement money from those who bow out early can be used by the plaintiff's lawyers to finance their fight against the defendants who decide to tough it out.

A Legal Lottery

But the wild card, and the most infuriating aspect in all of these cases, is that for the alleged victims and defendants alike, the system of awarding punitive damages has turned into a legal lottery. A McDonald's customer spills supposedly scalding coffee in her lap and is awarded $2.9 million by an Albuquerque jury. Yet someone could be maimed for life and receive only minimal damages if he or she gets an unsympathetic jury, a bad lawyer—or both.

Plaintiffs lawyers argue that punitive damages are awarded in only a relative handful of cases and that the headline-grabbing damage awards are typically reduced on appeal (as happened to the one against McDonald's). True. But this ignores that 95 percent of defective-product and personal-injury cases are settled out of court and not subject to appeal. And since punitive damages are sought in most cases, the fear of a seven-figure judgment by a maniacal jury can drive up the cost of negotiated settlements.

Even if a jury's award is overturned, the protracted appeals process clogs the court system and tends only to increase the billable hours of the lawyers involved—not put money in the hands of victims. A study by the management firm Towers Perrin found that the U.S. tort system returns less than 50 cents on the dollar to the people it is designed to help—and returns less than 25 cents on the dollar to compensate for actual economic losses.

Limiting the amount of punitive damages would not only bring consistency to corporate punishment but also would prevent juries from dispensing awards based more on emotion than on reasoned consideration of the facts.

Says Schwartz, "Having a defined sentence will make punishment for corporate wrongdoers swifter, shorter and more equitable."

A System of Caution, Not Innovation

It would also move us away from an economic system that stresses caution and discourages risk-taking—a dangerous impediment to a productive and healthful society. A Conference Board study of corporate executives found that fear of liability suits had prompted 36 percent of the firms to discontinue a product and 30 percent to decide against introducing a new product.

Clearly, some of those products may have been dangerous and society no doubt benefited from the decision to pull them back. To be sure, a system that encourages recklessness, or that enables guilty companies to escape unpunished, would only make matters worse. But what we have now is a system that deprives defendants of due process while turning a random handful of victims into millionaires.

Changing things won't be easy. First, there is the enormous war chest of the trial lawyers, a group well known for contributing generously to the campaigns of politicians at both the national and state level. Second is the past success of opponents in framing tort reform as an issue that pits helpless, wheelchair-bound victims against wicked and deep-pocketed corporate titans.

In reality, we all pay the price for keeping the system as is: Whenever we buy a stepladder, or a pain killer or a car, the escalating costs of product liability are rolled into the bill.

It is easy, of course, to dismiss the reform efforts being taken up now as simple pandering to big business—much harder to look carefully at a flawed system and figure out how to improve it.

"Changes in tort law will in effect deny ordinary people access to a court system where their claims would be considered by a jury of their peers."

The Civil Justice System Does Not Need Reform

Joel Bleifuss

In the following viewpoint, Joel Bleifuss argues that the proposed reforms of the civil justice system would make it more difficult for people who have been wronged to sue negligent companies. American tort law protects the public against corporate wrongdoing by removing from the market such dangerous products as the Dalkon Shield and silicone breast implants, Bleifuss asserts. If the Republican-inspired changes are enacted, Bleifuss contends, businesses will be able to develop and sell harmful products with impunity. Bleifuss is an editor for *In These Times* magazine.

As you read, consider the following questions:

1. How are the current tort reform laws the last refuge for individuals, according to Ralph Nader, as cited by Bleifuss?
2. How does the annual cost of medical malpractice and product liability awards compare with corporate profits, according to the author?
3. How might a reformed civil justice system adversely affect Americans in the future, in Bleifuss's opinion?

Joel Bleifuss, "Civil Injustice," *In These Times*, February 20, 1995. Reprinted with permission.

Another week, another shackle. The latest legislative mana-
cle to issue forth from the Republican-dominated Congress [in
the spring of 1995] is a scheme that would restructure the civil
justice system so it conforms to the desires of bloodless corporations.

To that end, the GOP—in the name of freeing society from the
supposedly crippling legal costs of a suit-happy citizenry—is
proposing a series of "tort reforms" that would make it far more
difficult for individuals who have been wronged to sue negligent
companies. [The Product Liability Fairness Act, H.R. 956, was
passed by the House on March 10, 1995, and by the Senate on
May 10, 1995.]

I called [consumer advocate] Ralph Nader to ask what he
thought of so-called tort reform. He scolded me for using the
language of the enemy. "Here is a move to destroy tort law, and
they refer to it on our side as 'tort reform,'" chides Nader. He
suggests a few alternative terms, such as "tort deform," "the
wrongdoers protection bill," or "taking the judicial cop off the
corporate beat."

Nader defends the current civil justice system as the individual's last refuge in a society where corporate entities virtually
control both the legislative and regulatory processes. Through
tort cases filed in civil courts, the hormone DES, the Dalkon
Shield, silicone breast implants and various other unsafe products were all removed from the market.

"The tort system is a system of law that curbs and deters indus-
trial violence in the environment, workplace and marketplace,"
says Nader. "It compensates victims directly from wrongdoers,
instead of making the taxpayer pay for the health costs or the dis-
ability costs. It is not bureaucratized. The civil jury is the essence
of democracy. People who are aggrieved go to a lawyer, on a contingency fee, and if they win they change the law and improve
the safety of everybody in society. You would think this would
be a bastion of conservative commendation. But the Republicans' wrongdoer-protection bill just shows that these aren't conservatives, they are corporatists masquerading as conservatives."

The McDonald's Verdict

Of course, that isn't the way the press views the situation.
Most media outlets uncritically relay corporate PR [public rela-
tions] about juries that have forced corporations to pay enormous damages for seemingly trivial injuries.

Take the example of the $2.86 million a jury awarded in 1994
to an elderly woman in Albuquerque, N.M., who was badly
burned by a cup of McDonald's coffee. (A judge later reduced
that to $560,000.) Almost without exception, stories about the
case lampooned the woman's injuries and the size of the jury

award. Few asked why the jury slammed McDonald's. And thus this suit became another weapon in the corporate arsenal, another "fabricated, phony, incomplete anecdote," as Nader puts it.

The *Wall Street Journal*'s Andrea Gerlin was one of the few reporters to delve beneath the froth, into the facts of the case, which are: Stella Liebeck, 81, was sitting in her car adding cream and sugar to her McDonald's coffee, when she spilled the cup on her lap. The coffee was about 185 degrees, which is 20 degrees more than McDonald's competition. The coffee caused third-degree burns on her groin, thighs and buttocks. She spent seven days in the hospital and had to have skin grafts to repair the damage. Burns by McDonald's coffee are relatively common. From 1984 to 1994 the company has received about 700 complaints from customers who suffered burns—mild to third-degree—from spilled coffee.

Reprinted by permission of Mike Smith/*Las Vegas Sun*.

Apparently McDonald's thought Liebeck was a sitting duck. In court, company lawyers argued that the burn was the woman's fault because she failed to remove her underwear immediately. Further, McDonald's pointed out that the company should not be blamed because she was old and thus her skin was easily damaged. Then there was the McDonald's expert, hired for $15,000, who testified that the burns to Liebeck's groin from McDonald's coffee were statistically insignificant in light of the billions of cups of coffee that the burger behemoth serves up each year.

If spurious anecdotes are the weapons of choice for those who attack the civil courts, their straw men are trial lawyers—the attorneys who represent little old ladies suing corporations like McDonald's. Corporations talk as if trial lawyers are driving them into bankruptcy. But nationwide, only about $5 billion a year is paid out in medical malpractice and product liability claims. As Nader points out, that is less then the $5.3 billion in after-tax profits racked up in 1994 by one company, Ford.

Vital Protections at Stake

Most reporters have been content to report on this attack on the civil justice system as if it were just an intramural squabble between corporate CEOs and trial lawyers. Lost in this two-sided debate is the fact that vital public protections are at stake.

Ted Becker, a Chicago trial lawyer and former Yale sociology professor, says that the proposed changes in tort law will in effect deny ordinary people access to a court system where their claims would be considered by a jury of their peers. "Why not just do away with juries?" asks Becker. "That is the hidden agenda here. Then we can let corporations and insurance companies determine what a human life is worth, or what a person who is injured should be compensated. If corporations are really concerned about the increase in the size of jury verdicts in this country, they should put more effort into making products safe—and treating people fairly—and less effort into trying to influence the political process so that they won't have to do either of those things."

As it is, the current civil justice system is clumsy enough. Legal redress is still being denied to those who have suffered due to asbestos, dioxin-laden Agent Orange and exploding GMC trucks. The situation will only get worse under the judicial system being constructed by the GOP contractors. Let's consider a hypothetical horror story.

The New Civil Justice System?

It is 2008 and America's new civil justice system is in place. Thirteen years ago, the deregulatory initiatives proposed in the Contract with America became law, which eased the way for approval of a genetically engineered drug known as Porculant. It makes pigs grow bigger. Bigger pigs mean more bacon. And bigger profits for Sow Chemical, the drug's maker and marketer.

Back in 1995, the Food and Drug Administration (FDA)— hacked apart and then hastily reassembled—had only enough resources to do a cursory examination of the drug's effects. Their study concluded that Porculant was safe, but only in very small doses. Under new Republican rules, a "peer-review panel" of experts—which included Sow scientists—was convened and quickly approved the regulations the FDA had drawn up. By 1996, almost every pork product contained minute quantities of Porculant.

Twelve years pass, and lo and behold, as thousands of girls enter puberty they develop a rare form of breast cancer. The medical profession is mystified. But a few family physicians in the Ozarks—the buckle of the bacon belt—notice that the daughters of many hardscrabble farm families suffer from this rare type of breast cancer. They conclude that mothers of the afflicted girls were eating pork from hogs treated with Porculant when their daughters were in the womb.

A group of families with cancer-stricken daughters decides to sue Sow. But their legal options are extremely limited, thanks to the "reformed" civil justice system. Under the law, losers in civil suits must pay all the legal fees for both sides. And a long suit against Sow could cost millions of dollars—millions that the families don't have. Laws limiting the fees of trial lawyers have also been passed. Consequently, the families who want to sue have trouble finding a lawyer willing to risk years of work.

Success in the courts is also hampered by the fact that the new system of justice allows only "scientifically valid reasoning" to be introduced in court. Since eminent scientists on the peer-review panel have already approved the drug, the families rightly fear that the testimony from the environmental scientists supporting their case will not be heard.

Finally, the families realize they could have trouble suing Sow because they would have to offer "clear and convincing evidence" that Sow acted maliciously when it sent Porculant to market. In short, the future of a civil suit by the families is very much in doubt.

Although fictional, this scenario is not fantastical. It aptly demonstrates what the Republicans intend to accomplish with their so-called reforms: permit corporate pigs like Sow to treat the people of this country like so much swill.

"[A 'loser pays' rule] gives both defendants and plaintiffs strong new incentives to make and accept reasonable offers early in the process."

A "Loser Pays" Rule Would Deter Frivolous Lawsuits

Stephen Chapman

The same reasoning that holds corporations accountable for consumers' injuries should be applied to lawyers who file frivolous lawsuits, argues Stephen Chapman in the following viewpoint. Under the current system the winning party may still be financially devastated by a lawsuit's costs, he maintains. Requiring the losing party to pay the winner's legal fees would reduce dubious litigation, he asserts, and would encourage the opposing parties to settle out of court. A plaintiff or defendant who refuses to accept an offered settlement and then loses the case should be held accountable for the opposing party's legal costs, he contends. Chapman is a nationally syndicated columnist.

As you read, consider the following questions:

1. How did the U.S. House of Representatives alleviate worries about the financial risks of filing meritorious lawsuits, according to Chapman?
2. How would the "loser pays" rule benefit ordinary citizens, in the author's view?
3. According to Chapman, who are the only people who would not benefit from a "loser pays" rule?

Stephen Chapman, "Rationality Before the Bench," *Washington Times*, March 11, 1995. Reprinted by permission of Stephen Chapman and Creators Syndicate.

If I dump an unwanted load of garbage, sand, toxic waste, manure or anything else that constitutes a nuisance on your doorstep, you have a right to sue and force me to pay for all the trouble and expense I've put you to. Unless, that is, I dump a legal summons, in which case the trouble and expense all come out of your hide, not mine. You can win the lawsuit I filed and go bankrupt; I can lose and be out only a minimal amount.

Plaintiffs' lawyers, who make a living suing people, think corporations should be held strictly accountable for the injuries caused by their goods and services. If a pill harms someone, the manufacturer ought to compensate the injured person, even if the pill helped millions of others. There is considerable merit in this approach, at least within reason, because it forces companies to take great pains not to hurt anyone.

But by the same logic, suggests legal author Peter Huber, lawyers ought to be liable when they injure someone by filing an unjustified lawsuit. If a suit wins, they should be entitled to collect not only damages from the wrongdoer but the cost of suing him; if a suit loses, they should have to repair the damage wreaked on an innocent party.

If it makes sense to discourage bad products by making manufacturers pay, doesn't it make sense to establish similar incentives against bad lawsuits? "Why shouldn't lawyers be held to the same account as doctors, product manufacturers and all the other people they want to sue?" asks Mr. Huber.

The "Loser Pays" Rule

That's the question underlying one large piece of the House Republicans' 1995 civil litigation reform plan—known as "loser pays" [the Attorney Accountability Act, H.R. 988]. In its original form, it established a simple rule, followed to one extent or another in most of the world: If you lose, you pay the other side's attorneys' fees, up to the level of your own. The American Trial Lawyers Association (ATLA) objected on the grounds that this would "close the courthouse door" to sound and flimsy cases alike, since most people can't risk having to pay a large award if they lose.

Now it is refreshing to hear personal injury lawyers admit that expansive liability can deter not only wicked but virtuous conduct—just as it deters both good and bad contraceptives and good and bad football helmets. But they have a point. Most of us would hesitate to sue, even over a substantial injury, if we had to bet our home and life savings on the outcome. Many injustices might go uncorrected.

So the House scaled this provision back. Under the measure passed [by the House on March 7, 1995], a plaintiff would have to pay only if he rejected a settlement larger than the eventual award given by a jury.

Suppose X sues Y for $50,000, Y offers to pay $40,000, X insists on going to trial and a jury awards X $30,000—or rules against him entirely. X would have to pay Y's legal fees, but only from the time the offer was refused. Likewise, if a plaintiff offered a settlement and the defendant declined, the defendant would end up on the hook if he lost in court.

Quashing Extortion Suits

A major factor in the overlawyering of America is the frivolous lawsuit, filed in the hope of extorting a payoff—referred to as a settlement in the law's genteel parlance—from a defendant worried about the legal costs of lengthy proceedings, even though he knows he is in the right and would ultimately win. Conversely, rich defendants often use the threat of protracted proceedings to discourage legitimate claims. If the loser had to pay the legal fees of the winning party, both just claimants and just defendants would be encouraged, but unjust claims and unjust defenses would be discouraged. Thus, when John Q. Average had a strong case against Ajax Corporation, Ajax would not be tempted to run Average's legal bills into the stratosphere by protracting the proceedings because Ajax would know it will have to pay the plaintiff's fee when it loses the case. Similarly, extortion suits would be quashed because plaintiffs with lousy cases would be penalized with the opposition's costs—as they are now not—for bringing groundless cases to court. This would mean less work for lawyers and fewer of them. That has proven to be the case in England, which has "loser pays" rules—and only one third the number of lawyers per capita that we do.

Charles Peters, *Washington Monthly*, December 1992.

This approach removes most of the plausible worries about "loser pays," since it exposes the person suing to no financial risk unless he gets and refuses a settlement offer. People who have been injured wouldn't be deterred from seeking compensation. They would only be discouraged from wasting a court's time—and society's resources—once they have received a reasonable offer.

A Strong Incentive to Settle

The real beauty of this approach is that it gives both defendants and plaintiffs strong new incentives to make and accept reasonable offers early in the process, instead of fighting over every issue to the bitter end. If a claim has a serious chance of winning a $50,000 jury award, a defendant would be foolish to offer

$5,000—and could expect to pay handsomely for his obstinacy.

The pressure on both sides would be to converge at a sane middle ground, not to stake out extreme positions far apart. Frivolous suits would be discouraged—as well as frivolous defenses.

The trial lawyers' group portrays any change in the status quo as a heartless attack on the rights of ordinary citizens. But this one would improve the lot of many innocent victims. Currently, many comparatively minor injuries go uncompensated because lawyers, who generally are paid a share of the jury award, can't make enough to justify their time. If the injured person could collect for his attorneys' fees as well as damages, more lawyers would be willing to handle modest claims.

The bill approved by the House is the sort of reform that would reduce litigation without promoting hazardous products. Reducing litigation would be a boon not only to defendants but to legitimate plaintiffs, who would be better off getting quick compensation than enduring the ordeal of a lengthy court battle.

The only people who would be worse off are those with dubious claims—and their lawyers. This version of "loser pays" would reward sensible behavior, something our legal system could use more of.

"The 'loser pays' provision now gives a wealthy party or a corporate party the power to slam the courthouse door shut in the face of a working-class individual."

A "Loser Pays" Rule Would Deter Meritorious Lawsuits

John Conyers Jr.

John Conyers Jr. is a U.S. representative from Michigan. The following viewpoint is taken from a speech Conyers made before the House of Representatives on March 6, 1995. Conyers argues that a "loser pays" rule, which would require the loser of a civil lawsuit to pay the winner's attorney's fees, would benefit corporate America rather than the average American citizen. Many middle-income persons and small businesses would be deterred from filing reasonable claims because they would risk bankruptcy, he contends. However, Conyers maintains, corporations can deduct their legal costs as a business expense and therefore would still be able to file frivolous lawsuits.

As you read, consider the following questions:

1. How would the "loser pays" provision hurt the average citizen, in Conyers's opinion?
2. Why should Florida's experience with the English rule be a lesson to lawmakers, according to Conyers?

John Conyers Jr., "Should the House Pass H.R. 988, H.R. 1058, and H.R. 956, Legal Reform Legislation?" *Congressional Digest*, May 1995.

When the "loser pays" provision of the Attorney Accountability Act of 1995 (H.R. 988) was unveiled, it was part of the controversial *Contract With America* [a proposal of ten reforms advocated by the Republican-led Congress]. Now we know that H.R. 988 is really part of the Republican majority's contract with corporate America. And reading the fine print of this provision makes clear that the average American citizen is not a party to the *Contract*.

This bill, and all of the other bills we debated on civil justice reform, are drafted from a single point of view: the corporate defendant's. All these bills seek to cut out the plaintiffs' right to bring cases in the first place by either eliminating who you can sue, where you can sue, or how much you can receive in compensation for harm suffered.

If this bill really strived in a neutral fashion to penalize frivolous lawsuits, or to discourage the filing of clearly unmeritorious cases, no one in this chamber would have any trouble supporting this proposition.

But when the bill is clearly drafted to deter middle-income persons from pursuing reasonable claims in court and placing them at a severe disadvantage with risk-free parties, such as large corporations whose legal fees are normally deducted as a business expense, then I have great objection to this legislation.

We are told that the motivation behind the "loser pays" provision is the tremendous number of frivolous lawsuits filed every day in America. But the proponents offer no empirical data to support their claims. . . .

The so-called explosion in litigation through the 1980s and 1990s, upon reexamination, we find was brought by corporations suing other corporations or domestic relations suits. It was not an explosion of product liability actions or medical malpractice actions, or tort actions in general.

It is notable that the new majority of Republicans are eager to embrace the so-called English rule [the "loser pays" rule], just as prominent voices in England are calling increasingly for the abandonment of the rule in that country itself.

In a January 1995 editorial, [a] conservative British magazine called for the abandonment of the rule.

Deterring Reasonable Claims

This comes from England, not from the United States. It is clear that the "loser pays" provision in H.R. 988 fails to distinguish between frivolous cases and reasonable cases in which liability is closely contested, and thus will deter many, particularly middle-income citizens and small businesses, from pursuing reasonable claims for defenses.

As one scholar has noted, for a middle-income litigant facing some possibility of an adverse fee shift, defeat may wipe him out financially. The threat of having to pay the other side's fee can loom so intimidating in the mind of a person without considerable disposable assets that it deters the pursuit of even a fairly promising and substantial claim for defense.

A Double-or-Nothing Bet

The Common Sense Legal Reforms Act contains several provisions to deter plaintiffs from filing lawsuits, but the most chilling would force the loser in most civil actions to pay the costs of the winner, including legal bills. Corporations can afford to take the risk, but for someone already suffering an injury or loss, the provision makes the act of entering a courtroom more like a double-or-nothing bet at a poker table. Most have trouble paying their own legal bills, much less those of their opponents.

Jonathan Harr, *New York Times*, February 18, 1995.

It is intimidating to have such a proposal now brought before the Congress to become part of our law.

Middle-income parties and small businesses may have to place their very solvency on the line in order to pursue a meritorious claim. And frequently in tort cases we do not know what a meritorious claim is because the evidence might determine a case becoming a big winner or a total loser.

The Burden of Proof

The burden of proof in a civil case is preponderance of the evidence, often described as the amount of evidence that shifts the scale, if even only slightly, from the point of balance. A middle-income plaintiff confronted with a written offer to settle under Section 2 of this bill must settle at that point, unless he or she is willing to assume the risk of payment of the other side's attorney's fees, and for a middle-income plaintiff who would be financially ruined by such an award, the calculus becomes, in effect, whether it is reasonable beyond doubt that they will prevail.

That is a pretty high standard, and it is notable that the States, often referred to as the laboratories of democracy, have not in any significant numbers perceived the English rule to be an appropriate measure for their court systems, nor do I.

The Florida experience, in which doctors first demanded the English rule and then demanded that it be abolished, should be a reminder to us that unintended consequences often overtake the intended ones, particularly when we act hastily and without thoughtful deliberation.

The "loser pays" provision now gives a wealthy party or a corporate party the power to slam the courthouse door shut in the face of a working-class individual, or heaven help him if it is a poor individual, or an individual who was injured by the very claim that they are suing and seeking to get recompensed.

The proponents of the bill say that this measure will encourage the parties to settle, but our goal should not be to encourage the parties to settle at any cost. The goal should be to encourage reasonable settlements with all parties on a level playing field.

A Roll of the Dice

This bill encourages unreasonable settlements in cases where the liability is a close question and there is great economic disparity between the parties. We are now turning the negotiation into rolls of the dice; neither party can accurately predict what will happen if the case is a close one.

Remember, we are not talking about cases with no merit, or cases that have a clear potential. We are talking about close cases, and close cases are the ones that are being forced to be settled at any cost.

What we are suggesting in this bill in terms of whether someone should be punished for bringing a suit that may turn out to be meritorious is that people with no money must sit on their rights for fear that they will be totally bankrupted in the event they lose the suit. That is precisely what this bill is about. And if they hesitate for a lengthy enough period, the statute of limitations will kick in and their claim will have expired because it was not timely.

What is a working person to do? Forget a person that has no money and cannot even put up anything or lose their bank accounts or their home. But what about a working person gambling on pursuing a lawsuit if he could be exposed to paying both his attorney's fees and the defendant's fees? The answer is obvious; he is going to hesitate.

Why is it that we are going after working people? Someone earning $30,000 a year should not be caught up in the claim that the wave of litigation must now be somehow subsidized by making them pay attorney's fees of all parties in the event they do not succeed.

What if a person sought to become a plaintiff and thought that there was a 70–30 chance that he would prevail? Under the current law, a person could be very justified in determining to go forward. But under H.R. 988, he would be very prudent to hesitate and perhaps decide not to go, because he may not win. And why should he risk this huge loss under these circumstances?

(Editor's Note: The Attorney Accountability Act, H.R. 988, was passed by the House on March 7, 1995.)

"*Punitive damages are an anomaly in litigation,
since no one knows the parameters for a punitive
award.*"

Punitive Damage Awards Should Be Limited

Sherman Joyce

Sherman Joyce is the president of the American Tort Reform
Association, an organization that advocates changing America's
civil justice system. In the following viewpoint, Joyce argues
that manufacturers have withdrawn many safe and useful products from the market due to fears of product liability lawsuits
and exorbitant punitive damage awards. Because there are no
uniform standards establishing the amount of punitive damages
for particular situations, juries often award plaintiffs far more
than their injuries merit, he maintains. Limiting punitive damages would make the penalty equitable, Joyce contends, and ensure that the punishment matches the injury sustained.

As you read, consider the following questions:

1. What evidence does Joyce use to refute the claim that there is
   no litigation explosion?
2. How many punitive damage awards are reduced or
   overturned, according to the author?
3. How does the threat of punitive damages hamper settlement
   negotiations, in Joyce's opinion?

Excerpted from "Legal Eagles Prey on Malpractice Suits" by Sherman Joyce, *Insight*,
November 7, 1994. Reprinted with permission from *Insight*. Copyright 1995, The
Washington Times Corporation. All rights reserved.

The debate about reforming our system of damage awards in civil lawsuits is understandably passionate.

Critics of the system argue that sympathetic claimants are the beneficiaries of excessive awards because jurors, who always hail from the same community as the claimant, believe that justice will be served if the "deep-pocket" defendant is made to dig deep into that pocket. Defenders of the current system of torts (damages suffered by someone for which another person is legally liable) usually are lawyers who represent injured persons on a contingency-fee basis; this arrangement entitles them to receive a percentage of the jury award or settlement (usually one-third). They believe that any limitation on awards is inappropriate.

The System Fails

The real issue, however, is whether the current system deters misconduct while enhancing safety and providing fair compensation to injured persons in a timely fashion. Regrettably, the system fails badly in meeting these objectives.

It is beyond dispute that litigation in our society costs far too much and takes too long to conclude. According to the Senate Committee on Commerce, Science and Transportation, which for more than a decade has considered legislation to establish uniform national rules for product-liability law, cases take nearly three years to conclude once a suit is filed.

Opponents of tort reform argue that there is no "litigation explosion," but the facts speak otherwise. Plaintiffs with legitimate claims often settle for inadequate amounts because they cannot afford to wait years for compensation. Similarly, defendants who genuinely believe they would prevail on merits at trial often decide to settle a case because the costs of litigating would lead to a Pyrrhic victory at best.

Who can blame them? Stella Liebeck, an 81-year-old New Mexico woman, was awarded nearly $2.9 million in punitive damages because she spilled hot coffee she had purchased at the drive-up window of a McDonalds restaurant. The jury awarded her a sum equal to two days' coffee revenue for the parent company. Little wonder that attorneys frequently advise their clients to settle for an amount commonly referred to as "nuisance value."

Lest anyone think that the problems described above affect only lawyers, judges and litigants, witness the testimony presented at the May 20, 1994, hearing of the Senate Committee on Governmental Affairs on the liability of raw-material suppliers for medical-device manufacturers. The hearing, led by Connecticut Democrat Joseph Lieberman, provides a frightening assessment of the future of the implantable medical-device industry because of product-liability litigation.

Medical-device manufacturers face a critical shortage in the raw materials needed to make their products. The reason: Raw material suppliers have severely cut back production because their inclusion in product-liability lawsuits makes it a totally unacceptable risk. Du Pont has stopped marketing and distributing a type of polyester yarn used in artificial-heart valves even though its use as a component of medical devices represents a mere .002 percent of the overall market for the fiber. In the case of a defective jaw implant for which the company sold 5 cents worth of teflon for each unit, Du Pont spent $8 million defending itself under the doctrine of joint liability. The company since has reached the rational conclusion that supplying device manufacturers is not worth the risk.

But these decisions, no matter how sensible, have chilling implications for our society. Lifesaving medical devices will, as a result of product liability litigation, either be unavailable or in critically short supply.

Cruel and Unusual Punishment

Punitive damages are meant to punish—unlike compensatory damages, which are supposed to pay the victim for the full cost, economic and otherwise, of his injuries. This sort of penalty used to be reserved for "outrageous misconduct," but in recent decades the standard has been lowered considerably—which the awards most assuredly have not. The Rand Corp., a California think tank, looked at the Chicago courts and found that between the early 1960s and the early 1980s, the number of punitive damage verdicts rose 25-fold and the average award soared from $7,000 to $729,000.

What is it we are punishing? Not just awful misdeeds but socially valuable behavior. In a number of cases, corporations have been hung out to dry for conduct that was approved or even required by government regulators. Jury verdicts have driven from the market drugs and medical devices certified as safe and effective by the Food and Drug Administration.

Stephen Chapman, *Washington Times*, February 4, 1995.

One of the witnesses who appeared before the committee was Mark Reily of Houston. Reily was joined by his 9-year-old son, Thomas, who was diagnosed in infancy as suffering from hydrocephalus—water on the brain. Mark Reily recounted how the fluid buildup led Thomas to experience excruciating headaches as an infant. The condition subsequently was treated by the surgical insertion of a shunt, a drainage device without which the boy would have risked severe brain damage or death. Once the shunt was implanted, Thomas' condition improved dramatically and he began to live a normal life, until the shunt began to clog and had to be replaced. Since such devices must be replaced periodically, Thomas and thousands of children like him desperately need access to these products. Without significant legal changes, however, many people could lose access to lifesaving technologies. Lieberman warned that this problem will result in a public health crisis if it is not addressed promptly.

The problems posed by the tort system are not limited to suppliers of medical products. In the medical-technology arena, promising new treatments are not pursued for fear of unlimited liability. For example, Biogen, a biotechnology company in Cambridge, Mass., canceled plans to develop an AIDS vaccine. James Vincent, Biogen's chief executive officer, indicated that he was prepared to risk tens of millions of dollars on the project with the understanding that the company may never be able to develop a vaccine. He said that he was unwilling, however, to put such a product on the market in the current legal climate.

Vincent told the Senate Commerce Committee: "I have made a business judgment that there is a significant likelihood that the courts would bankrupt the company by awarding large judgments to sympathetic plaintiffs regardless of whether the vaccine actually caused the injury." Likewise, Abbott Laboratories canceled human trials of a drug that could prevent the transfer of HIV from a pregnant woman to her unborn child.

The excesses of the tort system are a problem for all businesses. A survey of corporate chief executive officers by the New York-based Conference Board, a business-research group, found that half of the companies surveyed had discontinued product lines for fear of excessive liability, and 39 percent decided not to introduce new products for the same reason. Further, 25 percent of those surveyed canceled research that could have resulted in new products.

Quasicriminal Penalties

Nowhere is the problem of unpredictability in civil litigation more apparent than in the process for awarding punitive damages, which are quasicriminal penalties awarded in civil lawsuits.

Punitive damages are an anomaly in litigation, since no one knows the parameters for a punitive award. By contrast, even violent criminals know what risks they face if they commit a crime. Most states that allow punitive damages provide little or no guidance to juries. That leaves it to trial judges and appellate courts to make some sense of a case. A study of punitive damages by the General Accounting Office found that half of all such awards are reduced or overturned altogether by the trial judge or on appeal.

The threat of punitive damages can severely hamper settlement negotiations. Good lawyers for both parties in a case generally can arrive at a settlement if they are motivated to conclude a matter without going to court. This prospect disappears, however, if the claimant or his or her lawyer is determined to receive punitive damages. If that happens, settlement negotiations generally break down, and the parties have to go through the time and expense of a trial.

The prospect of punitive damages also can have a chilling effect on the development of new, innovative products outside of the medical field. Aaron Twerski, a professor at Brooklyn Law School and one of the nation's leading scholars on tort law and product liability, told the Senate Commerce Committee that on many occasions he has advised corporations not to introduce certain products, even when they are sure the product is safe, for fear of punitive damages. He gives this advice even though he agrees that the chances of such an award are very small.

A fair and rational solution to the problem is a reasonable limit on punitive damages. The American College of Trial Lawyers, which is composed of a group of the nation's most accomplished and experienced litigators, has recommended that states, or the federal government, adopt a limit on punitive damages of two times the amount of compensatory damages or $250,000, whichever is greater. This is an important element of the effort to address the vagueness of the standards for assessing punitive damages and ensuring that there is some correlation between the injury suffered by the claimant and the amount of punitive damages. . . .

Tort Reform Is Necessary

The tort system must be reformed because it fails to adequately serve the interests of those it is intended to benefit. Rather, it benefits primarily those who administer it: lawyers. Only 40 to 46 percent of the costs of medical malpractice claims go to the injured parties. This is unacceptable. We can, and must, do better. Meaningful tort reform will reduce the delay and expense of litigation. It also will encourage the development of the best products that technology has to offer, reduce the cost of health care and ensure that essential medical services are readily available. Comprehensive tort reform is essential to meeting these worthy objectives.

"Punitive damages simply are not a factor in any but the rare product liability case, and have little effect on the business community."

Punitive Damage Awards Should Not Be Limited

Ernest F. Hollings

In the following viewpoint, Ernest F. Hollings refutes the benefits of limiting punitive damage awards as proposed in the Product Liability Fairness Act, a bill under consideration in the Senate in the spring of 1995. Hollings maintains that punitive damages are rarely awarded and have little negative effect on business. In addition, unlimited punitive damage awards help ensure that products on the market are safe for consumer use, he contends. Hollings is a Democratic senator from South Carolina.

As you read, consider the following questions:

1. What were the results of the punitive damages study by Daniels, as cited by Hollings?
2. Why should claims that punitive damages keep products off the market be dismissed, in the author's opinion?
3. According to Hollings, how does the Product Liability Fairness Act punish injuries to wealthy citizens more than injuries to poor citizens?

Excerpted from Ernest F. Hollings's remarks in the Minority Views of Senate Report 104-69, "Product Liability Fairness Act," on S. 565, submitted by the Senate Committee on Commerce, Science, and Transportation, 104th Cong., 1st sess. (April 18, 1995).

Once again, the Senate Committee on Commerce, Science, and Transportation has reported legislation to federalize our nation's product liability system. However, the 1995 version of the legislation is unwise, unnecessary, and without any factual basis. [The Product Liability Fairness Act, S. 565, has been passed by the House and Senate; as of November 1995 it is awaiting reconciliation.]

This measure would federalize an area of law that for over 200 years has been the province of the states. Such action should not be undertaken lightly or carelessly. Those who propose such dramatic change should, at a minimum, bear the burden of proving that such change is both warranted and likely to be effective. Unfortunately, however, the Committee has, once again, ordered this bill to be reported without requiring anything close to a demonstration that either factor is present. The factual record clearly shows that each stated basis for this legislation cannot withstand even minimal scrutiny.

Change Is Not Needed

Over the years the bill's supporters have asserted that the legislation is needed to curb the litigation explosion, improve the efficiency of the American jury system, remedy the liability insurance crisis, and to bolster American businesses' competitiveness. However, the Committee's work on this issue has clearly demonstrated that (1) there is no litigation explosion; (2) the current system generally works properly to fairly compensate injured victims; (3) the insurance crisis (which has now ended) was not due to product liability, but the underwriting practices of insurance companies; (4) the product liability system is not stifling American businesses' competitiveness; and (5) products kept off the market because of product liability concerns are not necessarily safe or innovative, but rather are examples of the system working properly to deter potentially dangerous products.

Thus, despite the supporters' claims, this bill will not make American business more competitive, will not create uniformity in the law, will not reduce insurance rates, and will not ensure more compensation for plaintiffs. Quite to the contrary, the bill will create considerable confusion within the courts, will precipitate more litigation, will have no effect on insurance rates, and will reduce the ability of injured victims to be compensated for their injuries.

The proponents claim that they want an efficient, fair, and predictable judicial system. However, they obviously are not aware that the American civil justice system, one of the most cherished institutions in the world, is rooted in a democratic jury system, where cases are decided on the facts and circumstances, not on profit motives.

If fairness and consistency are truly the proponents' goal, it is certainly not evident in the legislation. For example, one of the purported purposes of the legislation is uniformity, yet, the bill, for the most part, preempts state law only to the extent that the law favors consumers. Of course, state laws that are pro-defendant are left intact. Where is the uniformity in that?

Benefits of the Tort System

Those who defend the tort system argue that punitive damages are a powerful deterrent to corporate misconduct. As to criticism that the system primarily benefits "America's money-grubbing lawyers," as Republican Sen. Slade Gorton of Washington, co-sponsor of the Senate bill [the Product Liability Fairness Act], puts it, the proponents note that the contingency system rewards lawyers only when they win cases and ensures that even the poorest of victims have access to representation.

Stephen Gillers, a legal ethics professor at New York University Law School, says that in an era when Congress is attempting to cut back on the regulatory powers of government, the tort system assumes an even more critical role. If lawyers lose their incentive to take cases, "we are going to leave people without adequate remedies," he says.

Gene Kimmelman, a co-director of Consumers Union's Washington office, says the fear of punitive damage awards without limit creates "a stronger incentive than the marketplace itself to ensure that manufacturers are careful about putting dangerous products on the market, or withdraw them as soon as they learn of the dangers."

Trial lawyers note that judges don't hesitate to reduce verdicts that seem too high: Thirty of the 72 jury verdicts in 1994 for $10 million or more were reduced, set aside or found to be essentially uncollectible, according to the National Law Journal.

Benjamin Weiser, *Washington Post National Weekly Edition*, October 9–15, 1995.

The bill raises the standard of proof for punitive damages to clear and convincing evidence of conscious, flagrant misconduct, but also protects companies that engage in such conduct through arbitrary damage caps. Not only are the damage caps arbitrary, they are applied in a manner that discriminates against non-wealthy citizens. The bill provides that punitive damages are limited to three times economic damages, or $250,000, whichever is greater. So, the greater a plaintiff's wealth, the more a company will be punished. Or to put it simply, injuries to wealthy citizens are more punishable than injuries to working-class citizens. This is completely contrary to the purpose behind punitive damages—namely, to punish outrageous conduct. . . .

Few Punitive Damage Awards

Much has been made of the unpredictability of results in product liability trials. However, it has been recognized, as it must be, that most of this is due to our jury system. I cannot believe any of my colleagues want to tamper with that system. When a product liability case goes to trial, the jury is not impaneled for the purpose of giving away someone else's money. Rather it is charged with the administration of justice. These juries are composed of our friends and neighbors, who conclude, some of the time, that the defective products involved and the injuries sustained require compensation. And it is our friends and neighbors—who work for a living and know the value of a dollar—who occasionally conclude that punitive damages are justified when the defendant has engaged in outrageous behavior.

If there is an issue that has been terribly exaggerated in this debate, it is the issue of punitive damages. Much new data is available on punitive damages, which show, among other things, that very few punitive damage awards have been made in all state and federal product liability cases over the last 25 years. Punitive damages simply are not a factor in any but the rare product liability case, and have little effect on the business community. Dr. Stephen Daniels of the American Bar Foundation conducted a nationwide study of over 25,000 civil jury awards between 1981 and 1985. The study found that punitive damages were awarded in only 4.9% of the cases reviewed. He stated that the debate over punitive damages "changed in the 1980s as a part of an intense, well-organized, and well-financed political campaign by interest groups seeking fundamental reforms in the civil justice system benefiting themselves." He went on to state that this "politicization of the punitive damages debate . . . makes the debate more emotional and manipulative, and less reasoned. The reformers appeal to emotions, fear, and anxiety in this political effort while avoiding reason and rational discourse."

He concluded that punitive damages were not routinely awarded, were awarded typically in modest amounts, and were awarded more often in financial and property harm cases [business v. business] than in product liability cases. His research also pointed up the errors in the data from Cook County, Illinois, and San Francisco, California, which in the past have been cited by supporters of bills like S. 565 [the Product Liability Fairness Act] as indicative of the nationwide pattern on punitive damages. He found that there were flaws in the method of data analysis used, and that it was inappropriate in any event to generalize from data in two counties to a nationwide trend.

On April 4, 1995, Dr. Daniels, testifying before the Committee, submitted data on a study he conducted to review his initial findings. Using the same database in a review of the same sites for years 1988–1990, he found that punitive damages were again awarded at an extremely low rate—4.8%. The study confirmed his earlier findings that such awards are more of an aberration than the norm.

Another Similar Finding

Dr. Daniels' findings are similar to those by Professor Michael Rustad of Suffolk University Law School and Professor Thomas Koening of Northeastern University, both in Boston. The Supreme Court recently referred to this report as "the most exhaustive study of punitive damages." Professors Rustad and Koening reviewed all product liability awards from 1965–1990 in both state and federal courts. During that time, punitive damages were awarded in only 355 cases—only 355 total punitive damages in 25 years! One quarter of all those awards involved one product—asbestos. Another one quarter of those cases was reversed or remanded upon appeal. They further found that the amount of punitive damage awards was not skyrocketing, and in 35 percent of the cases in which punitive damages were awarded they were less than the amount of compensatory damages. They concluded that "[t]here is a widespread misperception that punitive damage awards are skyrocketing because of frivolous lawsuits."

As witnesses testified at the Committee's September 23, 1993 hearing, if a manufacturer is not engaged in flagrant disregard of safety, pursuant to the standard set under section 107 of the bill, then that manufacturer does not have to be concerned about punitive damages. The possibility of punitive damages provides an important deterrent which helps to insure that manufacturers police themselves. We must require continued maximum vigilance from the manufacturers themselves. In its 1993 decision in *TXO Production v. Alliance Resources*, the Supreme Court soundly rejected attempts to limit or abolish punitive damages. . . .

Encouraging Safety Innovations

Another popular argument made in support of the bill is that the current system deters innovation, and discourages new products from being brought to market. Of course, this effect is, by its nature, somewhat subjective and very difficult to examine. However, witnesses at the Committee's hearings that examined the effects of the tort system on the chemical industry noted that desirable innovation must mean safe innovation, and that if the tort system discourages unsafe innovation, that is valuable. They also found that, even in the chemical industry in which manufacturers pay a minuscule percentage of the costs of the injuries caused by their products, the tort system works to encourage the innovation of safer products.

Punitive Damage Caps Are Unfair

[Punitive] damage caps, which limit an injured consumer's award to a predetermined amount, are arbitrary and capricious. Unlike a jury, which can weigh facts and tailor an appropriate award, a cap blindly applies regardless of the nature and severity of the injured party's pain and suffering.

If a 62-year-old insurance agent must rely on dialysis for the rest of his life because doctors removed his healthy kidney instead of the diseased one, is it fair that his jury award is slashed by California's $250,000 cap?

Is it fair to reduce the jury award to a limit of $430,000 for an 8-year-old Missouri girl who sustains brain damage and blindness as a result of her doctor's negligence during surgery?

Is it fair to reduce an award of $1.2 million to $500,000 for the survivors of a 50-year-old pipe fitter who died as a result of a doctor's misdiagnosis?

Such cases illustrate the insidious nature of damage caps. Juries, who hear all of the evidence and are in the best position to determine the seriousness of the damage to an injured consumer, are stripped of their role as evaluators of just compensation. Moreover, caps allow the wrongdoer to avoid responsibility for the harm he or she has caused.

Larry S. Stewart, *Insight*, November 7, 1994.

Business can, and often does, say it is discouraged from bringing innovative products to market, but it does not say what those products were, so the claim cannot be analyzed. However, those actual products that have been cited by witnesses in support of this claim subsequently had legitimate questions raised about their safety. In such cases, until such questions are resolved, I do not think we should presume that the product liability system has not worked properly to keep those products from the market. . . .

A Substantively Flawed Bill

Section 107 of the bill is cited as "Uniform Standards For Award of Punitive Damages." By including such standards, the bill's supporters are acknowledging that such damages are important in deterring outrageous and unacceptable behavior by manufacturers. However, by its terms, it applies to punitive damages only "if otherwise permitted by applicable law." Thus, in states which have, through state law, eliminated or limited punitive damages, this bill would not restore the availability of such damages. In some states, there would be no right to punitive damages; in some states they would be capped at a stated amount; and they would be available only if the burden of proof in this legislation is met. This clearly does not, and is not intended to, create uniformity in the law of punitive damages. If proponents truly wanted uniformity, and were serious about deterring egregious conduct, they, at a minimum, would restore punitive damages in the states that have limited them so that the law would be consistent nationwide. As Professor Lucinda Finley of the Buffalo School of Law, stated in testimony before the Committee on April 4, 1995, "to advance the goal of uniformity, punitive damages ought to be equally available to injured people without regard to what state they reside in."

Section 107 also caps punitive damages at three times economic damages or $250,000, whichever is greater. This standard will have the effect of permitting persons with higher economic losses (e.g., wages, business opportunities), to collect more in punitive damages than persons with lower economic losses. The implied message, of course, is that injuries to persons with higher incomes and salaries (i.e., wealthy citizens) should be punished more than harm caused to lower-wage earners (i.e., working-class citizens or women who are homemakers). . . .

Legislation Is Not Necessary

I regret that the Committee has once again proceeded to report legislation to federalize product liability tort law without any comprehensive data to demonstrate (1) that the legislation is necessary, and (2) that the legislation will work. The evidence is clear that this legislation will not have its purported effect of making the civil justice system more efficient or enhancing the competitiveness of American businesses. Our nation's civil justice system is one of the most admired systems of justice in the world. It should be cherished and preserved, not tinkered with, or modified in the interest of singularly self-interested groups.

I believe that, before the Congress delves into this area, it should seek the guidance of the majority of state legislatures and judges, who have handled such matters for over 200 years, as well as legal experts. I did so, and they all gave a resounding "no" to this legislation. We would do well to listen to them.

Periodical Bibliography

The following articles have been selected to supplement the diverse views presented in this chapter. Addresses are provided for periodicals not indexed in the *Readers' Guide to Periodical Literature*, the *Alternative Press Index*, or the *Social Sciences Index*.

ABA Journal	"Public Discontent," August 1995. Available from 750 N. Lake Shore Dr., Chicago, IL 60611.
Spencer Abraham and Mitch McConnell	"The Next Steps in Real Tort Reform," *Washington Times*, May 3, 1995. Available from Reprints, Washington Times, 3600 New York Ave. NE, Washington, DC 20002.
Anita Blair and Larry Stewart	"Winners and Losers in the Tort Reform Arena," *Washington Times*, April 2, 1995.
Carl T. Bogus	"The Contract and the Consumer," *American Prospect*, Spring 1995. Available from PO Box 383080, Cambridge, MA 02238.
John S. DeMott	"Product-Liability Reform . . . Maybe," *Nation's Business*, April 1995.
Maggie Gallagher	"The Law on Their Side," *New York Times*, June 12, 1995.
Mark M. Hager and Ned Miltenberg	"Punitive Damages and the Free Market," *Trial*, September 1995.
Peter Huber	"Liability Lies," *Forbes*, March 13, 1995.
Anthony Lewis	"Tort and Retort: Should We Make Litigants Pay for the Court Cases They Lose?" *Washington Monthly*, May 1993.
Jonathan S. Massey	"Why Tradition Supports Punitive Damages," *Trial*, September 1995.
Peter Nye	"Surge of SLAPP Suits Chills Public Debate," *Public Citizen*, Summer 1994.
Larry S. Stewart	"Damage Caps Add to Pain and Suffering," *Insight*, November 7, 1994. Available from 3600 New York Ave. NE, Washington, DC 20002.
Robert Wright	"Tortellini," *New Republic*, March 20, 1995.
Hiller B. Zobel	"In Love with Lawsuits: Why Litigiousness Is a National Character Trait," *American Heritage*, November 1994.

Is There a Litigation Explosion?

The
Legal
System

Chapter Preface

Dow Corning, a manufacturer whose breast implant was just one of its 8,700 silicone products, contends it was forced into bankruptcy in May 1995 due to litigation against the company. Facing a class-action lawsuit brought by 90,000 women who claim silicone-filled breast implants made them sick, Dow Corning agreed to a $4.2 billion settlement in March 1994. Five months later, the number of women in the class grew to 146,000. When the number expanded to over 400,000 women in May 1995, Dow Corning filed for bankruptcy.

Dow Corning's bankruptcy is used as an example by politicians and others who claim that Americans are overly litigious. For example, Christopher Cox, a Republican state senator in California, claims that American consumers are behind a litigation explosion that is driving companies out of business. Most companies cannot afford the high legal costs involved in defending themselves against frivolous lawsuits, he maintains, and many companies are forced to either file bankruptcy or else lay off workers and raise prices to stay solvent—all of which destroys America's economic growth and competitiveness, according to Cox. In order to reduce the number of such lawsuits, Cox advocates sanctioning attorneys who file the suits and forcing losers in lawsuits to pay the winners' attorney's fees.

Others argue that America is not besieged by a litigation explosion, nor would reforming the legal system reduce the number of lawsuits in the civil courts. Ralph Nader, a prominent consumer advocate, maintains that Americans do not take advantage of their right to sue and punish corporate wrongdoers. He asserts that only 10 percent of those who are injured by a defective product file a lawsuit seeking compensation for their injuries. Similarly, in a 1995 study, the National Center for State Courts, a judicial research organization, found that 61 percent of the lawsuits filed in civil courts in 1993 were traffic cases. Reforming tort laws by requiring losers of lawsuits to pay the winners' attorney's fees would not reduce the civil court caseloads, the center maintains.

The arguments supporting and denying the existence of a litigation explosion are buttressed with facts and statistics backing up each point of view. The authors in the following chapter examine whether America is too litigious and whether the number of lawyers and lawsuits needs to be reduced.

"More and more Americans are suing and getting sued on flimsier and flimsier grounds every year."

America Is Experiencing a Litigation Explosion

R. Emmett Tyrrell Jr.

The United States has become a more litigious country, R. Emmett Tyrrell Jr., editor in chief of the conservative periodical *American Spectator*, argues in the following viewpoint. The courts are overwhelmed with frivolous lawsuits that are filed solely as a get-rich scheme by lawyers and malcontents, he maintains. Tort reform proposed by the Republican-led Congress will reduce the number of petty lawsuits filed, Tyrrell contends, and ease Americans' fears of being a victim of a trivial lawsuit.

As you read, consider the following questions:

1. In Tyrrell's opinion, what reforms would reduce the frivolous lawsuits in America's legal system?
2. How do tort costs in the United States compare with tort costs in Japan, Germany, and the United Kingdom, according to the author?
3. How has Bill Clinton encouraged American litigiousness, in Tyrrell's view?

R. Emmett Tyrrell Jr., "Bucking the Tort Reform Tide," *Washington Times*, March 10, 1995. Reprinted by permission of the author.

President Bill Clinton may be the first American to go broke underestimating the intelligence of the American people. The cynic H.L. Mencken supposedly said that "No one ever went broke underestimating the intelligence or taste of the American people." Well, here comes Boy Clinton, the smartest young rascal ever to honeyfogle the gals and galoots of Hot Springs, Arkansas. His future solvency is in doubt.

Just the other day [in early 1995] at his press conference, he whined about how deplorably vulnerable his administration is to prosecution in the litigious atmosphere of Washington. Sure: He, his lovely wife Bruno, and a dozen or so of his appointees are being circled by a growing number of prosecutors, independent counsels, and other law enforcement agents, but the entire country has become litigious, not just Washington. "We live in a time now where the first thing people call for is a special counsel," said our leader midst a bewilderingly incoherent answer to a reporter's question as to why he is in so much legal hot water. [The Clintons and their business associates in Arkansas were being investigated for a real estate investment scandal known as Whitewater.] Yes, Mr. President, but you and your liberal friends have been the champions of the office of special counsels and of the poisonous atmosphere of litigiousness that engulfs us.

Fat and Happy Lawyers

Just three days after Mr. Clinton whined about the litigation he faces, his administration announced its campaign against the Republicans' efforts at tort reform. The GOP has promised to reduce the land mines of litigation that are concealed all around us, owing to the lawyers' hunger for perfect justice, out-of-court settlements, and gaudy contingency fees. The fees and settlements have made trial lawyers fat and happy, at least until they get hit by a bad day in court. More and more Americans are suing and getting sued on flimsier and flimsier grounds every year. The courts are choked with frivolous suits triggered by some malcontent's fanciful complaint or by some lawyer's scheme to get rich. Both prosper on the misery of others, and the misery need not be all that serious. Remember the lady who sued McDonald's because she spilled its hot coffee on her fibula, or perhaps tibia, whilst riding in a car and holding the coffee between her thighs. A jury awarded her nearly three million for that, and her lawyer moved on to the next lunkhead, or perhaps he retired.

The Republicans want the losers in frivolous or nuisance suits to pay the legal costs they have imposed on their opponents—or shall we say their victims. The Republicans want punitive damages to be brought back to earth, and they want to keep scientific frauds out of the courtroom. They want to return the courts to the dignified constitutional tribunals that they were, rather than the gambling casinos that trial lawyers have turned them into. The lawyers gamble with the law and we all pick up the tab. Tort costs as a percentage of Gross National Product amount to less than one-half percent in Japan and about one-half percent in Germany and the United Kingdom. They have soared to over 2.5 percent of the American GNP. Everyone pays significantly higher insurance rates because of it. Plants that cannot keep up with skyrocketing insurance rates or are hit with exorbitant punitive damages are closed and jobs are lost. Yet the crafty trial lawyers prosper.

Reprinted by permission of Jerry Barnett/*Indianapolis News*.

Mr. Clinton (Yale Law School, 1973; husband of Hillary Rodham Clinton, Yale Law School, 1973) says the Republicans' reforms are a menace to "the average middle-class consumer" and a boon to the hellish "corporations" as though the "corporations" do not pass their costs of litigation, product liability insurance, and government regulation on to "the middle class consumer." From his chair as White House Counsel, the Hon. Abner Mikva (University of Chicago Law School, 1951) laments that "Basically, this is an anti-consumer set of bills." Apparently the Hon. Mr. Mikva is not aware that consumers also carry insurance, have to work in the business community, and live today with a fear of legal harassment that they never had to live with a generation ago.

Since the 1960s America has lived through an exponential growth in litigation expense. In California, the largest punitive damage awards affirmed on appeal were only $10,000 until the 1960s. In the 1960s the figure climbed to $250,000. It hit $750,000 in the 1970s. In the 1980s—hold on to your toupee, Mr. Mikva—it soared to $15,000,000! Now there is justice for you. The cost of litigation is climbing at 12 percent annually higher than the cost of health care that the White House was so exercised about in 1994. Yet Americans cannot avoid health care. They should be able to avoid rapacious lawyers and idiots who do not know that hot coffee ought not to be placed between the legs. They also ought to be able to avoid presidents who complain about a litigious society one day and encourage it a few days later.

> *"Lawsuits alleging injury have not risen substantially since 1985. Since 1990, the number of suits . . . even declined slightly."*

America Is Not Experiencing a Litigation Explosion

Maura Dolan

The problem with the American civil justice system, argues Maura Dolan in the following viewpoint, is not that there are too many lawsuits, but that plaintiffs are undercompensated for their injuries. Dolan contends that reforms of the civil justice system in California have prevented some claimants from receiving fair compensation. Many victims of malpractice or product malfunction never attempt to take legal action, she maintains. Dolan is the legal affairs writer for the *Los Angeles Times*.

As you read, consider the following questions:

1. Why is California's $250,000 cap on pain and suffering damages in medical malpractice cases unfair, in Dolan's opinion?
2. What has been the effect of California's "deep pockets" initiative, as reported by Dolan?
3. How many people who are injured by products or by negligent medical care take legal action, according to studies cited by the author?

The assault on the civil justice system was in full swing. Radio and television ads denounced greedy lawyers and depicted rescue workers as too afraid of being sued to do their jobs. Small business, the ads said, faced extinction because of lawsuits.

Part of an orchestrated campaign by business groups and others to limit personal injury suits, the 1995 media spots portrayed a litigation-crazed society that costs consumers millions and jeopardizes their safety. Law-makers in Sacramento, California, and Washington, D.C., pledged an overhaul.

No Exploding Crisis

But is an overhaul of the legal system really needed? Have personal injury and product liability lawsuits really exploded? Is the economy being hurt by trumped-up lawsuits? The numbers suggest trouble on some fronts, but no exploding crisis. In fact, lawsuits alleging injury have not risen substantially since 1985. Since 1990, the number of suits in the states that report them even declined slightly. A jury-verdict reporting service has also found that monetary awards have been falling since 1989.

The civil justice system is faulted by scholars not for giving huge amounts of money to unworthy litigants but for awarding too much for marginal injuries and too little for more serious losses.

"It's part of the folklore of our time," said Prof. Marc Galanter, director of the Institute for Legal Studies at the University of Wisconsin. "For whatever reason, people have focused on lawsuits as this horror hovering over them."

Americans have been just as litigious or more so in earlier periods of history, possibly because the legal system was cheaper to use, Galanter said. Citizens of the early Republic sued often, frequently over trivial amounts of money.

Clamoring for Relief

Clamor for restrictions on the freedom to sue and collect damages began after World War II and escalated when civil litigation exploded in the 1960s, after a historic ebb.

Society's authority figures—doctors, manufacturers, small business owners, school officials and prison wardens—felt the rising sting of lawsuits, and wanted relief.

"Suddenly all the managers and authorities in society felt they were exposed, that there was this new onerous accountability that was being imposed on them," Galanter said.

The laments culminated in 1995 in a flurry of legislative proposals in Washington and Sacramento. . . . California supporters of limitations also gathered signatures to place three lawsuit proposals on the state ballot in 1996.

While ads deplored suit-happy lawyers, the House in 1995 adopted a sweeping package that, among other things, would put a cap on pain and suffering damages for medical malpractice, limit punitive damages and assess non-economic damages in all civil litigation according to a defendant's proportion of fault. A bill passed by the Senate would limit damages in product liability cases. Both are headed for a conference committee.

Two of the measures passed by the House already have been tried in California with mixed results. The state's experience with them is instructive, suggesting that some claims by proponents may be exaggerated.

One of the measures, a $250,000 cap on pain and suffering damages in malpractice cases, has been touted as a way to help control national health care costs. Such a lid has been in place in California since 1975, but the state remains one of the most expensive for health care in the country.

The law treats injuries caused by the medical profession differently from those caused in other situations. Because of the cap on damages, a patient who sues a doctor or hospital is entitled to less compensation than a litigant suing over an identical injury caused in a traffic accident or other non-medical setting.

The California law also limits what lawyers can earn representing malpractice victims. Consumer activist Harvey Rosenfield, a fierce opponent of the measure, complains this has made it difficult for some to find attorneys to take their cases.

"The truth is patients have to sue, and pain and suffering is what pays the lawyers," agreed Harry Snyder, co-director of the West Coast regional office of Consumers Union. Snyder said the cap should "at least" be raised to $700,000 to reflect inflation since 1975.

California doctors, however, probably have benefited from the malpractice cap. Their malpractice premiums have grown at a slower pace than the national average.

"I wouldn't be in business if it weren't for the [California] law," said Dr. George Koenig, a Redwood City neurosurgeon.

In his 24 years of practice, Koenig said he has been sued "two or three" times and settled "one or two for nuisance value." He estimated that his malpractice insurance costs about $30,000 a year.

A Just Law?

The cost of insurance, however, obscures what for some is the more important question: Is the law just?

Suzanne Lobb, still grieving for her husband, says it prevented her from adequately punishing [the health maintenance organization] Kaiser Permanente for his July 1993 death. Dwight Lobb, 47, succumbed to internal bleeding after undergoing elective surgery at a San Diego Kaiser facility.

Although internal bleeding was known to be a risk, nurses failed to put him on a monitor after his operation, heed his complaints of excruciating pain or call a doctor for his plummeting blood pressure, his widow said.

Hospital records showed he had been left unattended for 90 minutes despite the evidence of complications, she said. A medical examiner found he died of blood loss and advised his son-in-law, a police officer, to hire a lawyer.

Kaiser paid a $400,000 settlement, including the maximum $250,000 allowed by state law for pain and suffering. Lobb kept $128,000 and gave $150,000 to her two children: a gift from her husband, who had always hoped to help his children buy their first homes. The rest went to cover legal and funeral costs.

More money would not have eased her grief, but it might have assuaged her anger.

"I felt if I could hurt them financially, I could get their attention and make them change," she said bitterly.

Trischa O'Hanlon, senior counsel for Kaiser, said the hospital admitted "errors were made that we seriously regret," moved quickly to settle the case and took undisclosed steps to prevent a recurrence.

"We recognized there was a problem. . . . " O'Hanlon said. "Human error can happen anywhere. And unfortunately in medicine, when it does occur, at times the result can be devastating."

Little Impact

In addition to the malpractice measure, California's 1986 "deep pockets" initiative also would be embodied in national law under the House-passed legislation. County governments in California had backed the ballot measure in hopes it would curb skyrocketing insurance premiums.

The initiative, Proposition 51, limited the amount defendants must pay for pain and suffering, emotional distress and other non-economic damages to their proportion of fault. If the most culpable defendant is broke, the party that was only partially responsible for the injury can no longer be required to pay all the emotional distress damages. Damages for lost wages and medical bills were not affected.

But county governments that supported the measure now are uncertain whether it reduced their liability costs, and an ongoing study has yet to find any impact on jury awards.

Its effect so far has "probably been minimal," said Los Angeles County Counsel Robert Ambrose, because it only changed liability for non-economic damages.

Nor did the law entice the insurance industry back into the

market for local governments, said Michael Fleming, general manager of an authority that pools insurance for counties.

"The insurance companies really withdrew from the market in about 1985," Fleming said, "and for the most part they haven't really come back."

The effect of Proposition 51 has been "nil, zero," said Consumer Union's Snyder, because juries were not hitting the counties with excessive awards prior to the measure's passage.

Some Have Benefited

But the measure limited the liability of counties and other defendants, even if it did not lower premiums, and some defendants have clearly benefited.

Kevin Dunne, who defends companies sued for product liability, pointed to a recent case in which a woman sued a lawn mower manufacturer after she suffered disfiguring burns. Dunne, a San Francisco lawyer, represented the lawn mower company.

The woman's husband had filled the lawn mower with gasoline but had trouble starting the machine. He had a mechanical background and decided he could fix it with some help from his wife.

His tinkering left his wife with burns over almost half her body, Dunne said. The victim argued that the product should have contained warnings about the potential dangers.

"Without Proposition 51, we could never have argued his negligence," Dunne said. "With it, we could argue he [the husband] was a significant factor in causing the accident."

The case was settled. The amount is supposed to be confidential, but Dunne said it was "significantly less than seven figures." Without the law, the settlement probably would have exceeded $1 million, he said.

Legitimate Complaints Underrepresented in Court

The deep pockets measure and other lawsuit limitations are aimed at reducing liability, but the problems with the civil justice system are more complex, scholars maintain. They say litigants with questionable injuries tend to collect too much money while those with legitimate injuries get too little or do not even use the system.

A 1990 Harvard University study examined injuries caused by negligent medical care in New York. Less than 10% of those believed by a medical panel to have been injured because of malpractice took legal action. Similarly, a RAND study found that fewer than 5% of people injured by a product consult a lawyer.

"There is significant evidence that the system pays too many non-meritorious claims . . . while people with serious injuries can't get adequate compensation," said Deborah Hensler, director of the Santa Monica think tank's Institute for Civil Justice.

She cited a RAND study that found one-third of insurance claims in 1993 for auto accident–related medical costs were inflated or fraudulent, contributing to higher premiums and medical costs.

The rate at which such claims are filed has been rising about 4% a year, faster than the rise in population, said Hensler, whose organization receives about a third of its money from the insurance industry.

Mass personal injury litigation also is rising and may deliver some victims too much and others too little, Hensler said. She cited the burst of litigation over breast implants.

Many claimants contend the implants gave them connective tissue diseases such as rheumatoid arthritis. But epidemiological studies have been unable to link such illnesses to the implants. Some women have experienced no ill effects but have filed claims anyway as a precautionary measure.

This means that a $4.23-billion settlement must be shared by 400,000 claimants, reducing what the neediest of women will receive and jeopardizing the future of the agreement.

Another problem is the cost of compensating people through the civil justice system. A RAND study in the early 1980s found that 61 cents of every dollar spent on asbestos litigation went into the pockets of lawyers.

"It costs about a dollar to move a dollar in the tort system," Galanter said, "and Social Security can do it for 6 cents."

Some victims who deserve compensation may not get access to the courts because of the costs, analysts say. In some class action lawsuits, the biggest winners are the lawyers. Defendants often try to settle such suits by throwing money at the plaintiffs' lawyer instead of directing it to the class of aggrieved litigants.

"To the extent that some of the consumer groups say the system doesn't need fixing, I think they are wrong," RAND's Hensler said. "But the question is what the fixes should be, and it isn't clear to me that some of the proposals from the business sector will fix the real problems."

"Contemptible people filing frivolous lawsuits with the help of unscrupulous lawyers are delaying legitimate lawsuits by up to 10 years!"

Consumers Overburden the Courts with Frivolous Lawsuits

Edward Grimsley and Paul Harvey

In Part I of the following two-part viewpoint, editor and nationally syndicated columnist Edward Grimsley argues that frivolous lawsuits are overloading the legal system. He contends that Americans no longer take responsibility for the consequences of their own actions but try to put the blame for their problems on anyone who may have a connection—no matter how remote—to the case. In Part II, nationally syndicated columnist Paul Harvey maintains that many lawsuits filed by prisoners and consumers are frivolous and a waste of the courts' time. These unnecessary lawsuits are a drag on an already overburdened justice system, he asserts, and cause a lengthy delay in the resolution of legitimate lawsuits.

As you read, consider the following questions:

1. What is the They-Made-Me-Do-It theory, according to Grimsley?
2. Why are there so many lawyers, in Grimsley's opinion?
3. What solution does Harvey suggest to ease the number of frivolous lawsuits filed in court?

I

From the Census Bureau comes word that America has three times as many lawyers as firefighters. Well, of course. When a house burns, the owner will find a lawyer to be at least three times as useful as a firefighter.

Firefighters can only extinguish the blaze and contain the damage. But lawyers can help the homeowner with the more important task of pursuing potentially lucrative lawsuits against a variety of people who might be blamed for the fire and related problems. This is why the first telephone call a prudent homeowner will make when he discovers that his house is on fire will be not to the neighborhood fire station but to his lawyer.

A fire generates a host of complex legal questions. The homeowner and his attorney must decide whether to sue the builder, the realtor who negotiated the sale, the previous owner or all three. Since faulty wiring often causes fires, the homeowner must consider the possibility of suing the electrical contractor who wired the house. And he should never overlook the firm that installed the furnace. If fire department inspectors determine that the fire was started by a smoldering cigarette the homeowner had dropped into the crevices of a sofa, he will surely sue the tobacco company. Had it not manufactured the cigarette, would there have been a fire?

On the way out of his burning house, the homeowner should sniff for the presence of toxic fumes. It is always possible to sue the manufacturers of insulation, carpets, furniture and other objects that might emit dangerous smoke and gases.

In fleeing the fire, the homeowner's most direct path to safety might be across his neighbor's yard. If he falls into the neighbor's swimming pool in the process, he should resolve to sue the neighbor, as well as the company that installed the pool. The fleeing homeowner's chances of winning a handsome sum will rise dramatically if the neighbor's dog bites him as he climbs from the swimming pool.

There was a time, long ago, when a house fire could be dealt with simply by pouring water on it. That was the heyday of the firefighter. But fires obviously have been complicated by the growing tendency of people to blame all of their troubles on the malice and carelessness of others. It is becoming foolishly old-fashioned for an individual to admit any responsibility for the difficulties he might encounter in life.

The They-Made-Me-Do-It Theory

This was illustrated by a lawsuit that was reaching its climax even as the Census Bureau was announcing its findings on lawyers and firefighters. It involved a man who had developed lung cancer after smoking almost two packs of cigarettes a day for years, even though he was aware of the health warnings on the package. Contending it was the tobacco company's fault that he had persisted in smoking, he sued for damages. The jury rejected his claim, but several other such cases are pending; and some lawyers predict that very soon now a jury somewhere will rule against a tobacco company and encourage a flood of such cases.

This notion that an individual can collect damages for the adverse consequences of doing something he knows to be potentially dangerous is based partly on what could be called the They-Made-Me-Do-It theory. The essence of the theory is that the victim would not have used a damaging product if the manufacturer had not given him an enticing opportunity to do so.

On this theory, a driver who maimed himself by smashing his car into a tree at 90 miles per hour could sue the automobile manufacturer for (a) producing a car capable of going that fast and (b) stressing the glamour of speed in its advertisements and commercials. Naturally he could also sue the highway department for allowing a tree to grow at that particular location.

Someone Must Pay

Our summer softball game is a minor victim of the litigation explosion. In the mid-1980s, when lawsuits seemed to be quadrupling and insurance companies were therefore quintupling everyone's premium to pay for all this commotion, the park where we play decided that each regular activity on its premises had to be separately insured. . . .

So our little pickup game pays $772 in insurance for 20 mornings of play. As I read the policy, it does not cover any of the players—only spectators. . . . Why can't someone who decides to watch a game of middle-aged softball assume the risk of an occasional conking by a foul ball?

Answer: Because that's not the way things work in the world's most litigious society. Everything bad that happens to us is someone else's fault, and someone else must be made to pay, even if we really fund all this litigation ourselves through higher prices and higher insurance costs.

John Leo, *U.S. News & World Report*, May 22, 1995.

An alcoholic could sue a beer manufacturer on grounds that he overindulged only because the brewer's thirst-provoking advertisements and television commercials sent him back to the refrigerator for beer after beer despite his wife's warning that he was drinking too much. If he lost his temper and struck her, she could file her own suit against the brewer.

Companies found to be liable because advertisements for their products proved to be irresistible might recover some of their losses by suing their advertising agencies for being too persuasive. This would raise serious questions about freedom of speech and press, triggering the need for even more lawyers.

Some people blame lawyers for the litigation explosion, but that is unfair. All of those interest groups—environmentalists, consumer activists, health zealots, feminists, children's advocates and others—that are lobbying for laws and legal penalties to promote their causes are to blame also. It is only natural that the legal profession would expand to meet the growing need for lawyers. Indeed, it has a special obligation to do so. Given attorneys' commitment to the rule of law, there is no way they could justify violating the venerable old law of supply and demand.

II

You remember the McDonald's customer who collected 2.7 million dollars for spilling hot coffee on her lap.

You remember the New Jersey gardener who was sued by his neighbor for killing a rat.

And you remember the 360-pound lady who sued a movie theater because her "seat" was too small.

But do you recall the University of Idaho student who sued the college after falling out of his dorm window while "mooning" fellow students?

Or the murderer in Southern Michigan Prison, demanding his old job back as a high school teacher?

Or the New York City official who stole $200,000 of public money, wanting $8,500 more for unused time off?

Frivolous Prisoner Lawsuits

According to the United States Department of Justice, incarcerated criminals alone filed 30,000 lawsuits last year against prison officials. And, among the many dubious claims, there was one filed over the type of peanut butter inmates received—creamy vs. crunchy. Another was filed over a criminal's ice cream that melted before he could eat it, a third over the temperature of a toilet seat, a fourth about the lack of salad bars, a fifth over the limit of Kool-Aid refills, a sixth over the texture of scrambled eggs—and on and on and on.

Fully a fifth of the budget of the New York Attorney General's office is spent on prisoner lawsuits such as these.

What business do inmates have, having peanut butter, eggs, Kool Aid and toilet seats? What business do inmates have, having the ability to sue the society they sinned against? And what business does society have, listening to these and other trivial cases?

Contemptible people filing frivolous lawsuits with the help of unscrupulous lawyers are delaying legitimate lawsuits by up to 10 years!

A Good Start

As part of the Republicans' Contract with America [a proposal of ten reform bills backed by the Republican-led Congress in 1994–95], Rep. Jim Ramstad has sponsored a bill called the Common Sense Legal Reform Act [the House and Senate versions of the bill are awaiting reconciliation as of November 1995]. It may not be all that we need, but it seems a good start. If enacted, the bill will limit the amount of money sued for and it will force losers of many suits to pay the winner's legal fees.

That way, if some woman is foolish enough to hold hot coffee between her knees while riding in a car, or if some lady has eaten too many Milk Duds to fit into the standardized seats at a movie theater, or if some fellow is so unbalanced as to worry about the killing of a rat—he or she will think twice before risking the cost of his and everyone else's legal fees on a frivolous suit with only nominal returns.

"The volume of business suits far exceeds the number of cases filed by the victims of dangerous products and negligent medicine."

Businesses Overburden the Courts with Frivolous Lawsuits

Citizen Action

In the following viewpoint, the public interest group Citizen Action argues that the American Tort Reform Association (ATRA) and its business members have misrepresented the cause of overcrowded courtrooms. Although organizations such as ATRA blame consumer tort claims for clogging the court system, Citizen Action contends, frivolous business lawsuits are the actual root of the problem. Far more business lawsuits are filed than are consumer lawsuits for negligence or personal injury, according to a Citizen Action study. Therefore, the group maintains, tort reform will not lessen the courts' loads.

As you read, consider the following questions:

1. What percentage of cases in civil courts involve product liability and medical malpractice, according to Citizen Action?
2. Which companies filed the most lawsuits between 1991 and 1994, according to the public interest group?
3. What examples does Citizen Action give to back up its claims that frivolous business lawsuits clog the civil court system?

Excerpted from "Willful and Wanton Hypocrisy: Tort 'Reformers' Flood Courts with Lawsuits," a report from Citizen Action, April 1995. Reprinted with permission.

The primary proponents of restrictions [to cap punitive damages and limit product liability] include the most powerful corporations in the nation who work together through the American Tort Reform Association [ATRA] and the Product Liability Alliance. ATRA, the Alliance and their member companies claim that their proposals for limiting the civil justice system are necessary because "the volume of civil litigation, much of it unfounded and frivolous, is overwhelming our courtrooms."

The tort reform lobby and its political allies frequently make wild claims about the "explosion" of frivolous lawsuits by greedy patients and customers who "sue first and ask questions later" and cannot tell the difference between a "lawsuit on the one hand and a lottery ticket on the other." They claim such "frivolous, junk lawsuits" cost millions of dollars each year in higher product prices, medical costs, insurance premiums and taxes.

Such claims are nothing more than willful and wanton hypocrisy— the very corporations behind ATRA and the Product Liability Alliance are themselves responsible for a huge number of lawsuits. Many of these suits are filed against consumers and many against other businesses. Some of this litigation can only be described as "frivolous, junk lawsuits." The volume of business suits far exceeds the number of cases filed by the victims of dangerous products and negligent medicine.

While it may be in the interest of manufacturers and the medical industry to lower their financial liability for damage they may cause, this will do little to affect the amount or nature of most civil litigation. It *will* reduce the access to the courts and the adequacy of compensation to injured consumers. The proposals under consideration in Congress in 1995 constitute an attack on the fundamental legal rights of average Americans, but they will do nothing to reduce the number of frivolous suits or stem the tide of increasing civil litigation.

Tort Suits Just a Small Fraction

Court records show that only a small portion of all civil lawsuits involve tort cases. Data compiled by the National Center for State Courts for twenty-seven states found that only 9 percent of all civil filings were tort cases in 1992. As in preceding years, there were fewer total tort filings than contract suits, the latter generally filed by businesses. There were also fewer tort cases than in other major categories of civil litigation as well, including domestic relations and small claims cases.

In some of the nation's busiest court systems, the number of commercial suits greatly exceeded the number of tort filings. For example, over 59 percent of all civil cases in Cook County, Illinois's First Municipal District were contract disputes, while just 8 percent were tort cases in 1992.

Only a small percentage of all tort litigation involves product liability or medical malpractice cases. According to the National Center for State Courts' data from four states, just 4 percent of all tort filings in 1992 were product liability cases and just 7 percent were medical malpractice filings. This represents less than 1 percent of civil cases. Data from Illinois show a similar finding: just 0.35 percent of all Illinois civil filings in 1992 involved medical malpractice or product liability claims.

Compared to business contract suits, the number of such tort cases filed by injured consumers was minuscule. *The data indicates that there were ten times as many contract lawsuits filed in 1992 as suits involving both product liability* and *medical malpractice.*

Consumer Lawsuits Are Not Increasing

The total number of civil lawsuits *has* been increasing. Civil cases in all states increased 7 percent between 1990 and 1992 and were up nearly 25 percent over 1986. However, tort filings have not increased—the number of tort cases has been steady since 1986 and there were actually 2 percent fewer filings in 1992 than in 1990.

If the volume of civil litigation is overwhelming our courtrooms, it has nothing to do with the number of tort cases being filed. There is no evidence of any "lawsuit explosion" in tort filings, only a small percentage of which are initiated each year by consumers who have been harmed by negligent medicine or dangerous products.

One Lawsuit Every 12.5 Minutes

The members of the American Tort Reform Association and the Product Liability Alliance claim to oppose litigiousness and argue that the restrictions they support will reduce the number of lawsuits being filed. Yet these same companies themselves file a huge number of civil suits every year.

Computer records from courts in five states reveal that the members of ATRA and the Alliance filed almost 38,000 lawsuits from 1991 through 1994 just in the sixteen jurisdictions where online data is available: Illinois (Cook County), Florida (Orlando), California (Los Angeles, San Francisco, San Diego, Sacramento, San Bernadino, Santa Clara and Santa Barbara), New York ("selected city jurisdictions" including Manhattan, Bronx, Queens, Brooklyn, Nassau and Suffolk), and Pennsylvania (Philadelphia).

This is a minimal figure: these courthouses account for only 20 percent of all lawsuits filed in America. Nor does it count suits filed by many of the companies belonging to the industry trade groups and state tort reform organizations that fund ATRA or the Alliance, but are not identified as individual members.

Most of the suits filed by these companies were aimed at consumers—some 90 percent were actions taken against individuals. The remainder were filed against other businesses, including a number of instances where tort reformers were suing each other.

The companies that filed the most suits are well-known insurers, utility companies and manufacturers. State Farm Insurance headed up the list with over 11,700 suits, followed by Ameritech (5,009), Ford Motor (4,701), General Motors (3,068), Travelers Insurance (2,581), General Electric (1,887), Avco (1,871) and Liberty Mutual Insurance Company (1,268).

Over this four-year period (1991–94), the members of ATRA and the Product Liability Alliance filed an average of nearly 10,000 suits in these five states alone. Assuming the courts were open eight hours a day, five days a week except for holidays, this meant *the tort reform lobby was filing one lawsuit every 12.5 minutes that the courthouse doors were open.*

As noted above, this is an extremely conservative estimate. The total would be tens of thousands more each year if it included all the suits filed by all the companies funding the tort reform lobbying organizations. Taken together, the opponents of the "lawsuit explosion" are themselves filing suits every few minutes.

The Real McDonald's Lawsuit

Much has been made in the current debate over the "McDonald's case." The tort reform lobby has aired commercials across the country featuring the lawsuit against the fast-food giant by a New Mexico woman after she was scalded and received third-degree burns from a spilled cup of coffee. Supposedly the case symbolizes the "frivolous" litigation in our sue-happy society.

In fact, a much better example of lawsuit abuse in the civil justice system was an action taken by the McDonald's Corporation itself. *In October 1982, McDonald's filed a lawsuit in Miami federal court against its hamburger rival Burger King and sought a temporary restraining order to prevent broadcast advertisements that unfavorably compared the Big Mac to the Whopper.* Not to be outdone, Wendy's also filed a $25 million suit against Burger King for misleading advertising claims.

The docket of business-against-business litigation is filled with examples that can only be described as the type of "frivolous, junk lawsuits" so vitriolically denounced by the tort reform lobby. Many of these suits, of course, have been initiated by the corporations who fill the ranks of ATRA, the Product Liability Alliance, and their member trade groups. Ross E. Cheit detailed a number of such examples in a 1991 article published in *Studies in Law, Politics and Society*. Some examples include:

• In 1989, Uncle Ben's Inc. sued General Foods Corp. over advertisements claiming Minute Rice outperformed Uncle Ben's in the "slotted-spoon test."

• In 1989, the maker of Maalox antacid sued Procter & Gamble over ads promoting Pepto-Bismol as "an all purpose stomach medication."

• In 1989, Walt Disney Company used a lawsuit to force a public apology from the Academy of Motion Pictures Arts and Sciences for an "unflattering" representation of Snow White in the opening sequence of the 1989 Oscars ceremony.

• In 1987, in litigation between the makers of Tylenol and Advil involving false advertising claims, a court had to consider such important legal issues as whether Tylenol is "as effective" as Advil for headache pain and whether Tylenol is "unbeatable for headaches."

• In 1987, Kellogg filed a $100 million suit against General Mills, arguing that Post Natural Raisin Bran was not "natural" as advertised because it is coated with coconut oil and that comparative television ads were misleading because "extraneous material that would cling to the raisins had been cleaned off."

• In 1986, the producer of Minute Maid orange juice, Coca-Cola, sued Procter & Gamble, charging that ads for Citrus Hill Select "falsely" claimed that the juice was made from the "heart of the orange."

Lawsuits Filed by Businesses
Belonging to the Tort Reform Lobby

State	1991	1992	1993	1994	Total
California	1,548	1,639	1,576	1,925	6,688
Florida	995	1,633	1,446	1,229	5,303
Illinois	1,111	4,496	2,892	2,884	11,383
New York	4,135	3,431	2,450	2,630	12,646
Pennsylvania	897	577	307	197	1,978
TOTAL	8,686	11,776	8,671	8,865	37,998

Source: State Court Data Provided by Lexis

Citizen Action, "Willful and Wanton Hypocrisy: Tort 'Reforms' Flood Courts with Lawsuits," April 1995.

In addition to utilizing the civil justice system to mediate the hyperbole of product marketing, businesses also frequently sue over competing claims to brand names and corporate images. Some examples include:

• In 1989, Mead Corporation sued Toyota Lexus, claiming it

was attempting to capitalize on the Mead Data Corporation computer database "Lexis."

• In 1989, the Italian manufacturer of Beretta guns sued General Motors arguing that naming a car "Berreta" would "dilute" the gunmaker's good family name.

• In 1987, Regina Corporation charged in court that Hoover's Quik Broom II was "confusingly similar" to the Regina Electricbroom.

None of these frivolous civil actions will in any way be prevented or limited by the tort changes now under consideration in the Congress. The rights of consumers injured by medical malpractice and dangerous products would be drastically reduced, but our courtrooms will remain overwhelmed.

*"The country is losing [manufacturing superiority],
and litigation is one of the big reasons why."*

The Litigation Explosion
Has Made American
Business Less Competitive

Glenn W. Bailey

Litigation and the fear of lawsuits have caused almost half of all
U.S. manufacturers to stop production of or research on new
products, maintains the chairman of Keene Corporation, Glenn
W. Bailey. As a result of the litigation explosion and its ensuing
legal costs, American businesses are not as competitive as foreign corporations, he contends. If the legal system is not reformed, Bailey asserts, many businesses will go bankrupt defending themselves against lawsuits and thousands of workers
will therefore become unemployed.

As you read, consider the following questions:

1. According to Bailey, why is the tort system an inefficient way
   of distributing monetary compensation to plaintiffs?
2. What three reforms does Bailey suggest to keep businesses
   from going bankrupt so that plaintiffs receive their awards?
3. Why is consolidating cases counterproductive to limiting
   litigation, in the author's opinion?

Glenn W. Bailey, "Litigation Is Destroying American Companies," *USA Today* magazine,
January 1994; ©1994 Society for the Advancement of Education. Reprinted with permission.

A survey that was conducted by a Congressman among his constituents showed that, while most of them were concerned deeply about the economy, very few seemed to be worked up about America's competitiveness, even though competitive superiority in the world made the U.S. prosperous. The economy depends on it. Americans take U.S. manufacturing superiority for granted. However, the country is losing it, and litigation is one of the big reasons why.

Litigation impedes productivity. Forty-seven percent of the nation's manufacturers threw in the towel on some product they were making or planning to produce because lawyers have a chance to sue over a customer misusing the product or improperly handling it. Losses due to litigation might be endless, explaining why 25% of manufacturers discontinued some forms of product research and 15% laid off workers. Americans have forgotten that their rights are dependent on the willingness to take responsibility for their actions.

Compare Japanese and American cultures. The Japanese are motivated by a cooperative system that benefits all. A struggle for power in the Japanese culture is paramount. He who has the power, has the right.

Now look at Americans. They all ought to be proud of their individual rights, but, somewhere over the past decade or two, one's responsibility for his or her actions has been forgotten. People now look at power and perceive it as immoral. Americans say power works against the average person. How did that attitude come about? It's partly because we are becoming a nation of crybabies and busybodies, as an August, 1991, article in *Time* magazine stated.

Individuals forget their responsibilities, demand rights and entitlements, blame others for their problems, and don't want to pay for what happens to them as a result of their own actions. Lawyers exploit these trends and become rich. A number of them are obscenely greedy. As a result, the American civil justice system is breaking down, businesses are becoming less competitive, and jobs are disappearing.

Legalized Extortion

What exists today is a lawsuit lottery that leads to legalized extortion. Lawyers feed on the "entitlement generation" to create panic over asbestos and other products. Attorneys blame the suppliers of the products despite the fact that warnings on packages were ignored by workers, their unions, and their employers. Lawyers wrongly claim that suppliers were concerned about profits over people. They preach that they are taking from rich companies and giving to the poor, yet two-thirds of the money goes to attorneys.

A Roper poll of the American people reported in the *Wall Street Journal* showed that 70% agree that liability suits give lawyers more money than they deserve, and 63% agree that some people start frivolous lawsuits because the awards are so big and there's so little to lose. Almost 70% would limit punitive damage awards. By contrast, a survey of lawyers and judges also reported by the *Wall Street Journal* found that only 22% viewed the civil justice system negatively, while 77% blamed the media for clogging the courts and the breakdown of the system.

The *New York Times* reported that the American Bar Association rejects all limits on fact-finding before trial, appeals on convicted criminals, punitive damages, fees they charge, and so-called "junk science experts." Instead, the *Times* said, the ABA calls for more taxpayer funds for legal aid lawyers, tax benefits for payments to attorneys, a halt to Federal crime statutes, and additional judges appointed to handle more cases.

What has been the reaction to proposals for civil justice reform recommended by the President's Council on Competitiveness? Non-lawyers support them by 100 to one. Perhaps surprisingly, individual attorneys back the civil justice reform package by four to one. So, who's more in touch with reality, the public or America's largest organization of attorneys?

The fact is, lawyers are overwhelming America. The U.S. has one lawyer for every 300 people—about 70% of the world's attorneys—while Japan has one for every 10,000 of its population. With all of the lawyers we have in America, some of them have found it expedient to inspire panic to promote litigation through which they can build income for themselves.

Asbestos Litigation

Keene Corporation's experience with asbestos litigation is a perfect example of the civil justice system run amok as well as the negative effect litigation has on competitiveness. Keene bought Baldwin-Ehret-Hill in 1968 for $8,000,000. A small percentage of BEH's sales were in asbestos-containing products, made to meet U.S. Navy, utility, and construction project requirements. BEH placed warnings on its packaging before Keene purchased the company. In 1972, BEH stopped production of these products, which never produced a profit for Keene, and the company was shut down completely by 1975. Yet, despite this minimal involvement with a company it owned for a mere seven years, Keene is a major defendant in prohibitively expensive asbestos litigation.

Through 1992, Keene and its insurance carriers had spent about $415,000,000 on this litigation, even though the company never did anything illegal or improper. Keene has expressed willingness to provide total settlements up to $500,000,000—and lawyers will get more than $300,000,000 of that amount.

All of this has occurred even though it is undisputed that, when properly handled, asbestos products are safe and of great social utility. The U.S. Navy maintained as late as 1979 that it was impossible to build efficient naval vessels without asbestos.

While asbestos is number 90 on the Environmental Protection Agency's list of items that should concern people, asbestos litigation is number one as a cause of court clogging, number one in number of claimants, number one in causing bankruptcies of otherwise healthy and productive companies, and number one in generating lawyers' fees for damage litigation.

The Legal System and the Economy

Our system of civil justice is, at times, a self-inflicted competitive disadvantage.

Every year in America, individuals and businesses spend more than 80 billion dollars on direct litigation costs and higher insurance premiums. When you include the indirect costs, it may add up to more than 300 billion.

This is just one part of the problem. Look at the sheer number of disputes now flowing through our judicial system. One of the most insightful studies of the system is aptly titled *The Litigation Explosion*. In 1989 alone, more than 18 million civil suits were filed in this country—one for every ten adults—making us the most litigious society in the world. Once in court, many litigants face excessive delays—some caused by overloaded court dockets, others by adversaries seeking tactical advantage. In addition, many of the costs confronting our citizens are enormous, and often wholly unnecessary. And in resolving conflicts, Americans don't have enough access to avenues other than the formal process of litigation.

Dan Quayle, *Vital Speeches of the Day*, October 1, 1991.

The existing format for processing asbestos claims—through the tort system—is the most inefficient way to get money to claimants. In asbestos litigation, less than 35% of the funds go to the plaintiff. Because a system has evolved that establishes different legal standards for asbestos claimants—making it easier for unimpaired claimants to obtain grossly inflated damage awards—as few as five to 10 cents on the dollar are delivered to the truly impaired plaintiffs.

Judges' efforts to resolve cases all too often have resulted in a perverse incentive—causing more cases and more backlog. The opportunity for contingency fees that yield some attorneys returns of well over $5,000 per hour drive them to recruit more plaintiffs, many of whom are not sick. When cases are settled, these lawyers recruit still more plaintiffs and file still more cases, resulting in even more serious docket clogging and the further depletion of funds needed for truly impaired plaintiffs in the future.

Who Should Be Responsible?

Today's trials limit the plaintiffs' responsibility for ignoring warnings and the employer's responsibility for not providing a safe workplace and enforcing the company's then-existing requirement to wear respirators in areas where dust could not be controlled by the use of ventilation and dust collection equipment. Instead, they focus solely on the supplier and permit the introduction of irrelevant and inflammatory evidence, resulting in verdicts not related to the extent of the plaintiffs' injury, but to the heat of the lawyers' rhetoric. This combination inevitably leads to more cases and more trials.

Various cases yield unpredictable, inequitable, and arbitrary results. Juries, confronted with essentially the same facts, have awarded damages ranging from zero to millions of dollars! This "asbestos lottery" and its attendant high contingency fee payments have motivated plaintiff lawyers to recruit increasing numbers of unimpaired claimants to perpetuate their fee-feeding frenzy.

In some jurisdictions, defendants have been "gagged" from commenting on matters of public concern and presenting historical facts while judges and attorneys publicly have aired frequently prejudicial opinions.

Since the bankruptcy of Johns-Manville and other major suppliers, plaintiffs' law firms have scrambled to retool their practice and target smaller companies like BEH. The burden of larger and larger "lottery" type awards now falls on fewer and fewer companies with less and less money. For example, in a 1994 case, with 8,555 plaintiffs, approximately 85% of the 100-plus original defendants are not in the courtroom. Furthermore, though BEH had less than a few percent of the market and never mined or milled asbestos, Keene currently has more than 90,000 cases pending against it.

The asbestos litigation thus far has cost the American economy around $20,000,000,000, with about $12,000,000,000 going to lawyers. Those billions could have been used to invest in and create more than 200,000 jobs or 90,000 housing units.

Finding a Better System

If the goal is to run the litigation until every defendant has been bankrupted, thousands of people left uncompensated, and thousands of workers without jobs, then the legal system should continue what now is being done. On the other hand, if the goal is to do justice to the concerned parties and the public, what is needed is a system—uniform all over the U.S.—that will provide fair compensation to truly impaired plaintiffs promptly, stop unfounded new case filings, control transactional costs—mainly lawyers' fees, both plaintiff and defendant—and keep defendants in business to provide compensation for future meritorious claimants.

First, it is necessary to make sure that the money gets only to sick people. The best way to ensure that is by the establishment of court-mandated pleural registries, or some similar non-trial track docket. By establishing a pleural registry and ordering cases to it, judges could make the trial track litigation more manageable and unclog court dockets overnight.

A pleural registry would take the cases of all claimants who do not have any asbestos-associated impairment off the court's active docket and suspend the statute of limitations until the plaintiff becomes impaired. Only then would he or she have the right to return to court and have his or her case processed. It already is being done in some places, but to accomplish the above-stated goals, pleural registries must be implemented everywhere. Otherwise, there simply isn't enough money to pay these claims nor enough courts to process them.

Second, punitive damages must be stopped. Historically, they have been imposed on defendants as punishment for intentionally causing harm and as a deterrent to bad conduct. All punitive damage awards punish, but in the asbestos cases they don't act as a deterrent because these products haven't been made in decades and no harm was caused intentionally. What else can further awards of punitive damages deter?

Third, there must be a stop to consolidating cases, which is being used increasingly by trial judges to force settlements and control their dockets. This device actually is counterproductive and has resulted in a significant increase in the rate of new asbestos claims filed. Large consolidations make it impossible for a defendant to get a fair trial, resulting in inflated jury verdicts. That, in turn, creates more incentive to file more cases.

"American lawyers have not caused American consumers to buy Japanese cars, Italian shoes, and Korean videocassette players."

The Litigation Explosion Has Not Made American Business Less Competitive

Talbot D'Alemberte

In 1991, Dan Quayle, who was vice president under George Bush, publicly stated that the litigation explosion had hurt American business. The following viewpoint is excerpted from Talbot D'Alemberte's 1991 speech in which he responds to Quayle's allegation. D'Alemberte argues that lawyers do not have a negative impact on American competitiveness. Although the United States may have more lawyers and lawsuits than other nations, D'Alemberte maintains, America's inability to compete is due to capital, workforce, and technology problems rather than excessive litigation. Furthermore, he contends, the biggest increases in civil justice lawsuits were contract disputes—businesses suing other businesses. D'Alemberte, a former president of the American Bar Association, is the president of Florida State University in Tallahassee.

As you read, consider the following questions:

1. What problems have adversely affected America's economy, in the author's view?
2. According to D'Alemberte, what is responsible for the dramatic increase in tort cases?

Excerpted from "Civil Justice Reform, a Response to the Quayle Council" by Talbot D'Alemberte, *Vital Speeches of the Day*, March 1, 1992. Reprinted by permission of the author.

Thanks to Vice President [Dan] Quayle, we have a social and political context for our efforts to improve the civil justice system. His speech at [the American Bar Association (ABA)] annual meeting in August [1991] tapped a rich vein of public resentment of the legal profession.

It would be easy to dismiss the vice president's proposals as part of the narrow agenda of corporate special interest groups. But we should also applaud him for giving us the opportunity to bring attention to the real problems in our justice system and to accomplish genuine reforms. . . .

The vice president has charged that American lawyers are responsible for a litigation explosion which is clogging the courts and sapping our competitive strength. He has raised the specter of an economy hamstrung by unnecessary legal expenses and whole industries scared away from innovation by the threat of lawsuits.

Predictably, he received a good deal of attention for these attacks in our long national tradition of lawyer-bashing. But whom does he think he is kidding? Does he or any serious student of our competitiveness problem really believe that lawyers are responsible for our trade deficits?

Lawyers Are Not the Problem

American lawyers have not caused American consumers to buy Japanese cars, Italian shoes, and Korean videocassette players. Neither have American lawyers caused American businesses to buy German machine tools, Swedish electrical equipment, or Japanese electronic components.

Study after study of our economy detail the real problems—cost of capital, workforce skills, short-term management thinking, technology transfer diffusion. Nowhere do those studies single out lawyers as part of the competitiveness problem.

And if our legal system discourages innovation here, as the Quayle Council [the President's Council on Competitiveness] charged, why do foreign manufacturers out-innovate and out-compete American companies in American markets—where they must do business under the same laws American companies have to abide by? And why do more and more foreign manufacturers build factories and hire workers in America—exposing themselves even further to our legal system?

In other words, where's the so-called impact of lawyers on our competitiveness?

It simply doesn't exist, and I suggest that a council really dedicated to American competitiveness should propose real solutions to the real problems.

Yes, we have more lawyers. Yes, we have more lawsuits. And yes, we have problems with our civil justice system. But that's because America's unique commitment to individual rights includes the right to seek justice in the courts when all else fails. And the problems are justice problems, not competitiveness problems.

I don't know one critic who would trade our individual rights for those of individuals in countries like Japan, Germany or Korea—where the interests of big business and big government come first.

Lawyers Contribute to the Economy

The President's Commission on Competitiveness deplores the "baleful effects" of having too many lawyers. Vice President Dan Quayle and other politicians repeat the fiction that the U.S. has 70% of the world's lawyers, implying that this monstrous disproportion is responsible for flagging competitiveness.

On careful examination, the Bush-Quayle assertion that U.S. lawyers hurt our economy is wrong. . . .

A higher ratio of lawyers to white-collar workers is associated with *faster* rates of economic growth cross-nationally in the 1980s. In that decade, each additional lawyer per 1,000 white-collar workers produced a statistically significant 0.17% increase in annual per-capita GNP growth. . . . Lawyer populations did *not* impair growth after they reached a certain size. . . .

Lawyers contribute significantly to personal freedom and democracy—social goods that are missed in measures of economic performance. And in a complex, highly mobile society like ours, lawyers add value by devising ways for economic actors to achieve lower transaction costs in a context of imperfect information. Undoubtedly there are ways to provide legal services more efficiently and distribute them more fairly, but we can rest assured that America's high lawyer population has not undermined its economy.

Charles R. Epp, *Wall Street Journal*, July 9, 1992.

So let's all go beyond political potshots from both sides and get to work on the real challenge of civil justice reform. American lawyers are ready to cooperate and just as willing to adopt constructive reforms as anybody else.

In fact, we can welcome the raising of this issue before the public. It gives us an opportunity to highlight the ABA's work over many years to solve the problems of our civil justice system and to make clear what the real problems are.

We formed an ABA working group to gather up this extensive

past work and develop a detailed response to the Competitiveness Council proposals, with our own proposals, and we are submitting these to the Administration soon. We've met with congressional leaders, Department of Justice officials, and the vice president's staff to explain our position and find common ground with them.

Litigation Explosion Is a Myth

We've begun by showing that the so-called litigation explosion—the 18 million lawsuit cases filed in 1989, cited by the vice president—does not exist in reality. Eighty-two percent of those were traffic, criminal and juvenile cases. Of the remaining 18 percent, the vast majority are small claims, domestic relations, estate and contract matters.

The real subject of his criticism—tort cases—make up one-half of one percent of the total caseload in state courts. In federal courts, the number of new tort cases has been falling—not "spun out of control" as President George Bush said in October [1991]. The number of tort filings, except for asbestos cases, is down by 36 percent since 1984.

The National Center for State Courts earlier this year reported that tort case filings "are not increasing at a faster rate than other major categories of civil filings." Instead, it found that the most dramatic increases came from real property rights cases or contract cases—largely, corporations suing other corporations.

A similar study of federal courts found that suits between corporations rose 1,112 percent from 1971 to 1986.

As for huge punitive damages awards, a study supported by the Roscoe Pound Foundation found that the vast majority of U.S. manufacturers did not have a single punitive damage award against them in the past 25 years. It also found that, in the same 25 years, the proportion of million-dollar punitive damage verdicts has remained unchanged, when adjusted for inflation.

The real increases in litigation have come from businesses suing each other in contract and other disputes. In other words, the problems of big business with lawyers and lawsuits are largely self-inflicted. And the proposals of the Competitiveness Commission have nothing to do with this.

The Purpose of Punitive Damages

Let's also remember what punitive damages are for—to punish and discourage deliberate wrongdoing which cannot be punished any other way. With few exceptions, punitive damages went to victims of deliberate corporate decisions to trade safety for profits—and the lawsuits were necessary because government regulators were not doing their jobs of protecting the health and safety of the public.

For example, the decision against Ford Motor Company because gas tanks in the Pinto exploded when hit from behind. The company knew about the fatal design flaw. The company ignored it because of the cost of fixing the problem. The government did nothing. People died who didn't need to die. And going to court was the only way to stop the dying.

Or take the *Exxon Valdez* spill of 11 million gallons of oil into Prince William Sound, which oil companies assured us would never happen. Federal regulations were supposed to prevent such an environmental disaster, but the deregulatory binge of the last decade made those regulations ineffective. It was the lawyers for the victims and the courts who had to step in to force Exxon to pay for the damage it caused.

I'll cite a few more cases.

There were damages levied against a medical equipment company which failed to fix a polio victim's defective brace until it broke his leg. Incidentally, the punitive award in that case was $5,000, or ten times his $500 medical bill.

Other cases included a patient whose skin had to be scraped off because a supplier knowingly provided a hospital with contaminated surgical bandages—a baby food manufacturer who removed key nutrients from its product, causing brain damage to newborn babies—and a gas company which destroyed warning notices recalling defective gas fittings rather than mailing the warning to customers.

The High Costs of Accidents

As for costs which are a drag to our competitiveness, consider the huge cost of accidents in our nation. A major study by the Rand Corporation found that accidents in 1989 cost a total of $176 billion—nearly four percent of our gross national product. Just imagine how saving half or a quarter of that amount would improve our competitiveness.

While it might be tempting to believe that capping punitive damage awards will help competitiveness, remember that these would equally benefit foreign exporters to the United States. Many of the most important damage awards in recent years have been against foreign manufacturers such as Toyota, Honda, Volkswagen and Audi.

In fact, the only real effect of such caps would be to give the competitive edge to the least ethical manufacturer, domestic or foreign.

The plain fact is that our tort system is fundamentally sound. It can, and does, reverse on appeal many of the relatively few numbers of excessive jury awards, a reality ignored by the Competitiveness Council. In fact, a study of product liability cases found only 208 nationwide in the last 25 years which the Council's proposals would affect.

The same study found that punitive damage awards usually led manufacturers to make products safer and thus avoid future injuries or fatalities.

These and other court cases didn't happen because of lawsuit-happy litigators. They happened because federal safety and other regulatory agencies in the last decade have abdicated their responsibility to protect the public. This is a direct result of the deregulatory zeal of the Reagan and Bush Administrations in the service of big business and big money.

Weakening Safety Regulations

The Quayle Council today coordinates this campaign. It is the prime mover behind the weakening of worker safety, consumer product safety and automobile safety regulations, and the watering-down of environmental protections.

The Quayle Council continued this campaign most recently with proposed regulations that would leave unprotected half of the nation's wetlands, including major parts of such vital areas as Florida's Everglades and New Jersey's Pine Barrens.

Perhaps most disturbing, the council works in secret to thwart the Administrative Practices Act, which requires open regulatory decisionmaking. The only "outsiders" allowed have been corporate lobbyists. When asked for supporting materials or correspondence about its regulatory decisions, the council has refused, claiming "executive privilege."

Contrary to its name, the Competitiveness Council in its less than three years of existence has ignored the real causes of our competitiveness problem and worked exclusively to roll back regulations disliked by American manufacturers, corporate farmers and real estate developers.

Moreover, its efforts to roll back regulatory protections underscore the importance of civil suits with punitive damages as the last line of defense for most individuals—and the only way many safety advances ever happen. They are the symptoms of the failure of other branches of government, not the cause of some imagined injustice to corporate America.

Periodical Bibliography

The following articles have been selected to supplement the diverse views presented in this chapter. Addresses are provided for periodicals not indexed in the *Readers' Guide to Periodical Literature*, the *Alternative Press Index*, or the *Social Sciences Index*.

Dick Boland	"Suing for Fun and Profit," *Conservative Chronicle*, May 31, 1995. Available from PO Box 29, Hampton, IA 50441.
Lincoln Caplan	"Who Ya Gonna Call? 1-800-Sue Me," *Newsweek*, March 20, 1995.
Christopher Cox and Roberta Cooper Ramo	"Symposium: Is Public Hostility Toward Lawyers and the Legal System Justified?" *Insight*, November 13, 1995. Available from 3600 New York Ave. NE, Washington, DC 20002.
Michele Galen, Alice Cuneo, and David Greising	"Guilty!" *Business Week*, April 13, 1992.
Philip K. Howard	"The Death of Common Sense," *U.S. News & World Report*, January 30, 1995.
Diane McWhorter	"In Praise of Greedy Lawyers," *New York Times*, March 28, 1995.
Joseph Nocera	"Fatal Litigation," *Fortune*, October 16, 1995.
Jim Ramstad	"Common Sense Will Unclog Legal System," *Insight*, December 12, 1994.
Jonathan Rauch	"Growth of the Parasite Economy," *USA Today*, January 1995.
Thomas Sowell	"Legal Parasites Threaten System," *Conservative Chronicle*, May 31, 1995.
Catherine Yang	"Look Who's Talking Settlement," *Business Week*, July 18, 1994.
Catherine Yang	"Will the High Court Make Damages Less Punitive?" *Business Week*, March 15, 1993.

Is the Criminal Justice System Fair?

The
Legal
System

Chapter Preface

Dehundra Caldwell, a black 17-year-old honor student at Upson-Lee High School in Thomaston, Georgia, had no criminal record prior to August 1993. Neither did Sylvia Reed, a 52-year-old white woman and chief financial officer for Alternative Schools Network in Chicago. Caldwell was convicted of burglary after he admitted accompanying two other boys who broke into the high school in July 1993 and stole a box of ice cream bars worth $20. He was sentenced to three years in prison. Reed admitted to stealing $180,000 from her employer in August 1993. Her sentence was probation and 1,000 hours of community service.

Many blacks assert that the differences in the sentences between Caldwell and Reed illustrate the racism that is rampant in the American criminal justice system. Statistics show that although blacks represent only 12 percent of the U.S. population, they make up half the population in the nation's prisons. And a study released in October 1995 by the Sentencing Project, a Washington, D.C.-based organization that studies criminal justice issues and sentencing reform, found that 32.2 percent of black Americans are under the supervision of the criminal justice system. The Sentencing Project maintains that racism is a factor in the convictions of blacks on drug charges: "Blacks are arrested and confined in numbers grossly out of line with their use or sale of drugs," the report states.

While the criminal justice system may have discriminated against blacks in the past, it does not do so now, maintains Patrick A. Langan, a senior statistician with the U.S. Department of Justice's Bureau of Justice Statistics. He contends that a defendant's prior record and the seriousness of the offense have more of an influence on his or her arrest, prosecution, conviction, and sentencing than does the defendant's race. A study conducted by his department in 1993 found no significant disparities between the rates of prosecution and conviction of blacks and whites. Although this same study showed that more blacks were sentenced to prison than were whites, blacks committed more violent crimes and were more often repeat offenders, factors that judges strongly consider when handing down sentences.

Are blacks incarcerated at a higher rate than whites because of racism or because they commit more serious crimes? Does their imprisonment hurt or help the black community? The authors in the following chapter examine discrimination and fairness in the criminal justice system.

"A 1991 review of 700,000 criminal cases . . . showed that white defendants got better plea bargain deals than Latinos or blacks accused of similar crimes."

The Criminal Justice System Discriminates Against Blacks

Alan Ellis

Statistics show that blacks are treated more harshly by the criminal justice system than are whites, maintains Alan Ellis in the following viewpoint. Although whites sell and use most of the drugs sold in the United States, he asserts, blacks and Latinos are arrested and jailed at rates disproportionately higher than whites. Black and Latino crime victims do not receive equal justice, either, Ellis writes; their victimizers often receive more lenient sentences than those who commit crimes against whites. Until this racial disparity is eliminated, he concludes, blacks and Latinos will continue to vent their rage at their unequal treatment. Ellis, a lawyer in San Francisco, is the former president of the National Association of Criminal Defense Lawyers.

As you read, consider the following questions:

1. What evidence does Ellis present to support his contention that the criminal justice system discriminates against blacks?
2. How do the authorities disregard the constitutional rights of blacks and Latinos, according to Ellis?

Editorials following the violent reaction to the Rodney King verdict [in which blacks in south central Los Angeles rioted for three days after four white policemen were acquitted of using unnecessary force against black motorist Rodney King] laid the blame for the explosion on lousy schools, families without fathers, permissive attitudes toward drugs and sex, and last but not least, the minimum wage. The only recognition that the criminal justice system might be at fault is a call for a more "hard-headed juvenile justice system."

Discriminatory Laws and Practices

But the last thing we need is more hard-headed "tough on crime" rhetoric. Toughness is part of the problem.

Consider the following:

• A study by the National Center on Institutions and Alternatives found that 85 percent of all Washington, D.C., black males have been arrested at least once in their lifetimes.

• In a Memphis study on the excessive use of deadly force by police officers in pursuing suspects, it was learned that black suspects were 10 times more likely than white suspects to have been shot at by police officers, 18 times more likely to be wounded, and five times more likely to be killed.

• According to a 1989 survey by the National Institute on Drug Abuse, blacks made up 12 percent of drug users that year. But according to a *USA Today* article citing 1989 FBI figures, blacks accounted for 44 percent of all drug possession arrests.

• Under federal law, possession for personal use of five grams of crack cocaine (predominantly used by minorities) carries a five-year mandatory *minimum* sentence without parole. By contrast, such simple possession of any amount of powder cocaine, or any other drug, is a misdemeanor punishable by a *maximum* of one year.

• In Sacramento, where 70 percent of the people sent to prison for drug offenses are black, more than 63 percent of public drug treatment slots go to whites.

• A 1991 review of 700,000 criminal cases throughout the state of California showed that white defendants got better plea bargain deals than Latinos or blacks accused of similar crimes. The study also found that whites got more lenient sentences and went to prison less often.

In spite of the fact that whites sell most of the nation's drugs and account for most of its customers, it is blacks and Latinos who continue to fill up America's courtrooms and jails, largely because, in a political climate that demands a quick fix to the drug problem, their neighborhoods get treatment that would not be tolerated in more affluent, white areas.

Indeed, throughout America, blacks and Latinos report that

their neighborhoods have been barricaded by the authorities; that roadblocks, similar to those in South Africa, have been set up for "I.D. checks"; that the police roust them from their homes, without warrants or probable cause, to search for "evidence"; that they are targeted as part of police "stop on sight" policies, and that they are discriminatorily arrested in sweep operations for minor traffic violations.

This flagrant disregard for constitutional rights is causing a troubling phenomenon in cities across the nation.

Reprinted by permission: Tribune Media Services.

In New York, hundreds of black and Hispanic men have been caught in the New York Port Authority's drug courier interdiction net. Once a suspect has been targeted by Port Authority police as fitting a "drug courier profile," he is usually followed on board the bus, questioned, and eventually asked to permit a search of his bags. He is never told that he has the right to refuse. Of 210 people arrested in 1989, only one was white.

As New York Supreme Court Justice Carol Berkman aptly put it in one of her decisions on the issue, "Minorities did not fight their way up from the back of the bus just to be routinely stopped and interrogated on the way to the terminal."

In Boston, police have made a "substantial" number of unconstitutional stops and searches of black youths, including strip searches conducted on public streets, according to a report issued in December 1990 by Massachusetts Attorney General James M. Shannon.

According to this report, these illegal searches were a result of public statements by commanding officers that minority youths in certain areas of Boston, particularly individuals suspected as being associated with gangs, should be stopped and frisked or searched, regardless of whether they were engaging in illegal activity and regardless of their constitutional rights.

The Victim's Race

The race of the victim counts for something too:

• In Dallas, the rape of a white woman results in an average sentence of 10 years while the rapist of a Latino woman gets five years and the rapist of a black woman gets two years.

• Nationally, murderers with white victims are up to 4.3 times more likely to be sentenced to death than murderers with black victims.

The Rodney King beating, verdict and violent reaction should prod America to remedy discrimination in the criminal justice system. Such efforts need to be in the forefront of our national agenda.

A promising start would be the passage of legislation voted down in Congress in 1992 that would eliminate racial discrimination in the imposition of the death penalty. The Racial Justice Act would have permitted a challenge to a federal or state death sentence that furthers a racially discriminatory pattern of capital sentencing, in terms of either the race of the defendant or the race of the victim, based on statistical evidence.

Equally important would be prohibiting discriminatory, suspicionless dragnet sweeps permitted by the Supreme Court.

Racial Disparity and Incarceration

We would also do well to eliminate racial disparity in pre-trial detention. Black and Latino arrestees are far more likely than whites to be detained before trial. In Florida in 1989–90, blacks constituted 39 percent of felony marijuana cases but made up 58 percent of those detained before trial for that charge, according to a report by the Racial and Ethnic Bias Study Commission of the Florida Supreme Court. And, as any criminal lawyer knows, defendants who are incarcerated pre-trial are more likely to be convicted and to be sentenced to prison upon conviction.

Equal access to bail for all socio-economic classes requires that the amount of bail set be rationally tied to an individual defendant's actual resources.

And speaking of resources, non-indigent defendants can often, in effect, buy their way out of prison time through an array of valid sentencing alternatives. Sentencing specialists to help design effective and individualized alternative sentences are commonly unavailable to indigent defendants. Alternative sentencing planning services should be provided in every public defender office, and funding should be authorized for sentencing specialists to assist appointed counsel.

Until "equal justice for all" becomes a reality, the rage will continue and there will be more firestorms to come.

"The principal problem facing African-Americans in the context of criminal justice today is not over-enforcement but under-enforcement of the laws."

The Criminal Justice System Helps the Black Community

Randall Kennedy

In the following viewpoint, Randall Kennedy disputes the contention that blacks are treated unfairly by the criminal justice system. He argues that blacks face a greater likelihood of being victimized by black criminals than they do of being mistreated by the criminal justice system. Therefore, he concludes, the best way to help the black community is to arrest, prosecute, and imprison the black criminals. Punishing criminal conduct is a burden only to those who engage in illegal behavior, he contends. Kennedy is a law professor at Harvard University in Cambridge, Massachusetts.

As you read, consider the following questions:

1. What is the principal problem of criminal justice facing blacks today, in Kennedy's opinion?
2. In *State vs. Russell*, what justification did the state use to support stiffer sentences for crack than for powdered cocaine, according to the author?
3. How was the Minnesota Supreme Court misguided in its decision in the *State vs. Russell* case, in Kennedy's view?

Like many social ills, crime afflicts African-Americans with a special vengeance. African-Americans are considerably more likely than whites to be raped, robbed, assaulted and murdered. Many of those who seek to champion the interests of African-Americans, however, wrongly retard efforts to control criminality. They charge that the criminal justice system is (as it has been historically) an instrument of racist oppression. In all too many instances, their allegations are overblown and counterproductive; because they exaggerate racial prejudice in the criminal justice system, they detract attention from other problems of law enforcement that warrant more consideration.

Those who propound one-sided racial critiques of the criminal justice system maintain it is infected with a pervasive, systemic racial bias that targets black males. Depending on their age, they allude to bitter memories of the Scottsboro Boys [nine black teenagers who were convicted of raping two white women in Scottsboro, Alabama, in 1931, despite a retraction by one of the women] or Rodney King [a black motorist whose beating by four white Los Angeles policemen was captured on videotape in 1991. An all-white jury acquitted the police of using unnecessary force]. They portray police as colonial forces of occupation and prisons as centers of racist oppression.

Those who adopt this stance frequently proceed as if there existed no dramatic discontinuities in American history, as if there existed little difference between the practices that characterized the eras of slavery and *de jure* [legal] segregation and those prevalent today, as if African-Americans had completely failed in their efforts to reform and participate in government policy, and as if black legislators, mayors and chiefs of police did not exist.

The Danger Facing African-Americans

In fact, the principal problem facing African-Americans in the context of criminal justice today is not over-enforcement but under-enforcement of the laws. The most lethal danger facing African-Americans in their daily lives is not white, racist officials of the state, but private, violent criminals, typically black, who attack those most vulnerable to them without regard to racial identity.

Acknowledgment of these realities has given rise among blacks and others to an alternative to anachronistic racial critiques. This alternative perspective views criminal law enforcement as a public good, identifies primarily with the actual and potential victims of crime, and embraces policies that offer greater physical security to minority communities, even if that means ceding greater powers to law enforcement agencies and thus concomitantly narrowing the formal liberties that individuals currently enjoy.

Unfortunately, efforts to address the danger crime poses to minority communities are confused and hobbled by a reflexive, self-defeating resort by critics to charges of "racism." This often happens when a policy, racially neutral on its face, gives rise to racial disparities when applied.

An Intraracial Conflict

What is really at stake in many controversies with racial overtones is not simply an interracial dispute but an actual or incipient intraracial conflict. Although blacks subject to draconian punishment for crack possession are burdened by it, their black law-abiding neighbors are presumably helped by it (insofar as the statute deters drug traffic). Although black youngsters who wish to stay out late are burdened by a curfew, blacks who feel more secure because of the curfew are benefited. Although black members of violent gangs are burdened by police crackdowns on such gangs, blacks terrorized by these gangs are aided.

Randall Kennedy, *Wall Street Journal*, April 8, 1994.

Take drug policy. Some condemn as "genocide" the punitive "war on drugs" because a disproportionate number of those subjected to arrest, prosecution and incarceration for drug use are black. At the same time, others, including Rep. Charles Rangel (D., N.Y.) and Lee Brown, director of the Office of National Drug Control Policy, condemn proposals for decriminalizing drug use on the grounds that such policies would amount to genocide because racial minorities would constitute a disproportionate number of those allowed to pursue drug habits without deterrent intervention. These charges and countercharges of genocide are ridiculous.

State v. Russell

Overheated claims of racism also affect the judiciary. Consider, for example, the 1991 Minnesota Supreme Court case *State v. Russell*. In *Russell*, five African-American men were prosecuted for possessing crack cocaine and sentenced under a statute that penalized possession of crack more harshly than it penalized the possession of similar amounts of powdered cocaine. Possession of three grams of crack carried a penalty of 20 years in prison, while possession of an equal amount of powdered cocaine carried a maximum penalty of only five years in prison.

Mr. Russell and his co-defendants argued that no rational basis justified the difference in punishment. Moreover, they argued that this difference was racially discriminatory because it adversely affected, with insufficient justification, black cocaine users relative to their white counterparts. They based this argument on the fact that greater numbers of African-Americans use crack over powder. Statistics referred to by the state Supreme Court indicated that in Minnesota, in 1988, 96.6 percent of all persons charged with possession of crack were black, while 79.6 percent of all persons charged with possession of powdered cocaine were white.

The trial court invalidated Minnesota's sentencing scheme, and the Minnesota Supreme Court affirmed that decision, principally because of the racial disparities noted above. In the principal *Russell* opinion, Justice Rosalie E. Wahl wrote: "The correlation between race and the use of [crack] or powder and the gross disparity in resulting punishment cries out for closer scrutiny of the challenged laws."

The state justified its heavier punishment of crack possession on three grounds. First, crack and powder have different sociologies of use and distribution; dealing can be inferred from the possession of smaller amounts of crack. Second, crack has a more potent physiological impact. Third, more violence is associated with the distribution and use of crack.

Court Hostility

The Minnesota Supreme Court rejected these justifications and concluded that they failed to offer even a rational basis for punishing possession of crack more harshly than possession of powdered cocaine. The court dismissed testimony about the amounts of drugs that signaled dealing as opposed to mere possession as "purely anecdotal." The court also noted that, although crack is smoked and powder is inhaled, under certain circumstances the effect can be the same.

The Minnesota court's posture is that of a court scrutinizing a state policy with such intense hostility that its invalidation is virtually preordained.

In pursuing this course, the *Russell* court ignored the realities that have made the invention of crack a watershed in the history of illicit drugs. Although the court asserted that nothing substantial differentiates crack from powdered cocaine, the record before it indicated otherwise. Students of the drug trade note with awe the technological and marketing "advances" that distinguish crack—differences in pricing for instance, that enabled crack to democratize cocaine abuse and transform the illicit drug trade. In the 1980s, in the words of Mark A.R. Kleiman, "crack happened."

The court's hostility to the Minnesota sentencing statute stemmed from its perception that, in Justice Wahl's words, the law "appears to impose a substantially disproportionate burden" on blacks, "the very class of persons whose history [of oppression] inspired the principles of equal protection."

The court is misguided in two important respects: First, Justice Wahl's portrayal of Minnesota's sentencing statute as a "burden" to blacks as a class is simplistic. Assuming that one believes in criminalizing the distribution of crack cocaine, punishing this conduct is a public good. It is a "burden" on those who are convicted of engaging in this conduct. But it is presumably a benefit for the great mass of law-abiding people.

A Help or a Burden?

Many have observed that, all too frequently, politicians, newspaper editors and police officials express concern about crime only if they perceive that it inflicts injury upon whites.

This observation suggests a very different approach to the crack/powder distinction from that taken by the Minnesota Supreme Court. It suggests that we ought to commend rather than condemn the Legislature's distinction between crack and powdered cocaine. If it is true that blacks as a class are disproportionately victimized by the conduct punished by the statute at issue, then it follows that blacks as a class may be helped by measures reasonably thought to discourage such conduct.

In addition, the Minnesota Supreme Court condemned the statute as imposing an unjustifiable racially discriminatory burden. Yet to the extent that the heavier punishment for possession of crack falls upon blacks, it falls not upon blacks as a class but rather upon a subset of the black population—those in violation of the law who are apprehended.

Of course, laws that are apparently race-neutral can hurt blacks as a class. For example, one of the methods once used by Alabama to minimize the electoral power of blacks as a class was a state constitutional provision, silent on its face with respect to race, that permanently disenfranchised those convicted of committing certain crimes. In that instance, the delegates to the state constitutional convention openly admitted that the criminal law was purposefully being used as a weapon to disenfranchise blacks.

In *Russell*, by contrast, the court made no finding that the purpose of the Legislature's harsher punishment for possession of crack was to oppress blacks as a class. The court invalidated the Legislature's sentencing scheme because, even in the absence of discriminatory purpose, the law imposed what the court deemed an unduly burdensome effect on blacks. . . .

Being Wrong Is Not Racist

It is worth noting that, to an increasing extent across the political spectrum and within black communities, priority of sympathetic identification is flowing to victims as opposed to perpetrators of crime. Sometimes people with these sentiments become inhibited when they confront the paradox that increasing the extent and severity of crime control policy to protect law-abiding blacks will result in higher rates of incarceration and heavier punishments for black perpetrators, as most of those who commit crimes against blacks are themselves black.

Perhaps, however, they will come to accept that disparities like those in *Russell* may be the mark, not of a white-dominated state apparatus "discriminating" against blacks, but instead of a state apparatus responding sensibly to the desires of law-abiding people. This response may be wrong: Perhaps decriminalization would be better than continuing the war on drugs. But being wrong is different from being racist, and the difference is one that matters greatly.

"The cost of committing crimes is so shamelessly cheap that it fails to deter potential criminals."

Mandatory Minimum Sentences Are Fair

Phil Gramm

Mandatory minimum sentencing laws require judges to impose prescribed sentences for particular crimes rather than varying each sentence to fit the circumstances. In the following viewpoint, Phil Gramm argues that these laws are necessary because sentences for serious criminal offenses have become so lenient that lawbreakers have learned that crime pays. When would-be criminals know they will receive stiff sentences for their crime, he maintains, they are deterred from breaking the law. Mandatory minimum sentences keep drug pushers and other criminals off the streets and prevent them from terrorizing America, he asserts. Gramm is a Republican senator from Texas and is chairman of the Senate Subcommittee on Commerce, Justice, State, and Judiciary.

As you read, consider the following questions:

1. What is the main cause of the crime wave, in the author's opinion?
2. How has the expected punishment for a serious crime changed since 1950 as compared to the number of crimes committed, according to Morgan Reynolds, as cited by Gramm?
3. What is the distinction between a major and minor drug offense, in the author's view?

Two Federal judges announced that they would refuse to take drug cases because they oppose mandatory minimum sentences. One judge, Jack Weinstein of Brooklyn, confessed to a "sense of depression about much of the cruelty I have been party to in connection with the war on drugs." The other, Whitman Knapp of Manhattan, heartened that President Clinton "has not committed himself to the war on drugs in such a way as the Republican Administration had," hoped his action would influence the President to abandon tough mandatory sentencing.

If the Clinton Administration listens to these voices, and their echoes, and tries to roll back minimum mandatory sentences, it will certainly win applause from some criminal defense lawyers, judges and the media—and no doubt many criminals—but it will betray millions of Americans who took the President at his word when he promised to be tough on crime.

Contrary to conventional wisdom, most criminals are perfectly rational men and women. They don't commit crimes because they're in the grip of some irresistible impulse. They commit crimes because they think it pays. Unfortunately, in most cases they are right: In America today, crime *does* pay.

Morgan Reynolds, an economist at Texas A&M University, has calculated the amount of time that a person committing a serious crime in 1990—the last year for which we have complete statistics—could reasonably expect to spend in prison. By analyzing the probability of arrest, prosecution, conviction, imprisonment and the average actual sentence served by convicts for particular crimes, Professor Reynolds has reached some shocking conclusions.

On average, a person committing murder in the United States today can expect to spend only 1.8 years in prison. For rape, the expected punishment is 60 days. Expected time in prison is 23 days for robbery, 6.7 days for arson and 6.4 days for aggravated assault. And for stealing a car, a person can reasonably expect to spend just a day and a half in prison.

Given this extremely low rate of expected punishment, is it any wonder that our nation is deluged by a tidal wave of crime? In trying to account for the six million violent crimes committed annually, analysts point to the breakdown of the family, the effects of television violence and the failure to teach moral values in our schools. While these factors have an impact, they overlook the main culprit: a criminal justice system in which the cost of committing crimes is so shamelessly cheap that it fails to deter potential criminals.

Mandatory minimum sentences deal with this problem directly. When a potential criminal knows that if he is convicted he is *certain* to be sentenced, and his sentence is *certain* to be stiff, his cost-benefit calculus changes dramatically and his willingness to engage in criminal activity takes a nosedive.

Again, Professor Reynolds's statistics are revealing. He found that since 1950, the expected punishment for a serious criminal has declined by two-thirds, while the annual number of crimes has risen seven-fold. In 1950, each perpetrator of a serious crime risked, on average, 24 days in prison. By 1988, the amount of risked time was 8.5 days. Over 38 years, soft sentencing—treating criminals as victims of dysfunctional families, of predatory capitalism, of society at large—has brought a dramatic decline in the cost of committing a crime and a dramatic increase in crime.

Public Supports "Three-Strikes" Laws

An overwhelming majority of the public backs laws requiring life sentences without the possibility of parole for those convicted of three violent felonies, according to nationwide polls conducted by the *Los Angeles Times* in January and April 1994.

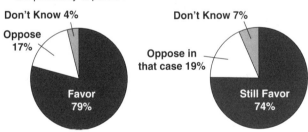

Do you favor or oppose a "three strikes and you're out" law, which requires any criminal convicted of three violent felonies to be imprisoned for life without the possibility of parole?

Don't Know 4%
Oppose 17%
Favor 79%

Would you favor the "three strikes and you're out" law even if it meant your state had to take money from other programs or raise your taxes in order to build new prisons?

Don't Know 7%
Oppose in that case 19%
Still Favor 74%

CQ Researcher, "Mandatory Sentencing," May 26, 1995.

Critics of mandatory minimum sentences point out, often with considerable indignation, that mandatory sentencing denies judges discretion in imposing sentences. And they are perfectly right. That's what we want.

Americans have lost faith in our criminal justice systems. Too many violent criminals have walked away with light or even no prison sentences. Mandatory minimum sentencing is a massive no-confidence vote by the American people in the discretionary powers of our judges. If judges and parole boards were legally liable for the actions of convicted felons who walk the streets due to their decisions, I would have more confidence in their judgment. But they are not.

"But what about fairness?" critics of mandatory minimum sentencing ask. "Is it fair that someone who has never committed a crime in his life should go to prison for 10 years because one day he sold drugs to some kid? Shouldn't we distinguish between a major drug dealer and a minor drug offense?"

Once again, the critics are right: There is a distinction between major and minor drug offenses. A minor drug offense takes place when a pusher sells drugs to somebody else's child; a major drug offense takes place when he pushes drugs on yours. Only when our nation's elites are as outraged about what happens to someone else's child as they would be were it happening to their own will we deal with crime effectively.

Of course, there is the cost issue to be considered. At a time when we are desperately trying to reduce the Federal deficit, can we really afford to sentence more criminals to jail for lengthier periods of time?

Of course we can. In 1990, the Department of Justice's bureau of statistics found that it costs from $15,000 to $30,000 to keep a felon in prison for a year. A Rand Corporation study calculated that the active street criminal imposes a financial cost of $430,000 a year on the general public—not to mention such immeasurable but very real costs as grief, fear and anger. By Washington standards (or anybody's, for that matter), spending $30,000 a year to save $430,000 a year is a brilliant allocation of resources.

In dealing with our nation's crime problem, cost is not the fundamental issue. Indifference is. I am appalled by the shoulder-shrugging approach some Americans take to the issue of crime in this country. Americans saw the pictures of starving children in Somalia and were outraged; we saw "ethnic cleansing" in Bosnia and were furious. But our outrage and fury evaporate when American children are the victims of criminals.

Like Judge Weinstein, all too many are ready to agonize over the "cruelty" that mandatory sentencing inflicts on drug pushers, and to overlook the cruelty that mandatory sentencing avoids by keeping these criminals off the streets and preventing them from brutalizing your children, mine or even Judge Weinstein's.

With the end of the cold war, domestic crime is now the greatest threat to the safety and well-being of Americans. And just as the U.S. developed a military strategy—"containment"—to deter Soviet aggression by raising its costs, so today we need a legal strategy to contain, and reverse, the growth of violent crime.

"Sentencing laws . . . mandate penalties that are on the face of it non-discriminatory, but that in operation are race-, gender-, youth-, and ignorance-biased."

Mandatory Minimum Sentences Are Unfair

Lois G. Forer

In the following viewpoint, Lois G. Forer argues that Americans' anger toward increasing crime has led to mandatory minimum sentencing laws, which require judges to impose tough, predetermined sentences regardless of the circumstances of the crime. She contends that these laws are unconstitutional, and that judges should be allowed to use their discretion when passing out sentences. Forer is a former trial judge and author of several books on the criminal justice system, including *A Rage to Punish*, from which this viewpoint is excerpted.

As you read, consider the following questions:

1. What reasons does Forer give for holding mandatory minimum sentencing laws unconstitutional?
2. Who is most affected by the mandatory minimum sentencing laws, according to Forer?
3. What are the unintended consequences of mandatory minimum sentencing laws, in the author's opinion?

Mandatory sentencing laws, guideline sentencing laws, and capital punishment . . . laws enacted since the mid-1970s have created a crisis situation. More than 1,300,000 persons are now imprisoned in the United States, a higher rate than in any other Western nation. The American crime rate is also higher than that of any other Western nation. Americans are spending more and more money every year on imprisonment but crime has not been reduced. Our streets, our schools, and our homes are not safe. The rage to punish persists. It is time to examine these failed policies and laws and to demand change.

I was moved to write this viewpoint because I have seen at first hand the cruelty and futility of American sentencing laws. For sixteen years I was a trial judge in Philadelphia, hearing all kinds of felony cases from car thefts to homicides. I left the bench when I was ordered by the Pennsylvania Supreme Court to impose a five-year prison sentence in compliance with a mandatory sentencing law on Michael S. He had not committed a violent crime; he had repaid the $50 he had stolen; he was employed, supporting his family, and had been arrest-free for more than five years. . . .

He was a young black man. He had been working steadily for more than a year but lost his job when the company moved. In desperation he held up a taxi with a toy pistol and took a total of $50 from the driver and passenger. No one was injured.

Michael was arrested a few days later. This incident occurred in 1983. A year later he was brought to trial before me. The evidence against him was overwhelming. I convicted him. That was the simple part of the case.

As was my practice, I ordered a presentence investigation. It disclosed that this was Michael's first adult offense; he had one juvenile offense. He was married and had one child. At the sentencing hearing I asked the driver and the passenger if they wished to speak.

Neither did. I then said that I intended to give Michael a short prison sentence, a long period of probation, and require him to repay the $50 after his release. Both the driver and the passenger said they thought the sentence was fair and appropriate.

An Unconstitutional Law

The prosecutor, however, demanded a sentence of five years total confinement under the state mandatory sentencing law. Like many other judges, I held the law unconstitutional for the following reasons:

1. It vested the sentencing power in the prosecutor not the judge, a violation of the separation of powers doctrine.
2. It abolished individualized sentencing. There were clearly mitigating circumstances: i.e., Michael's good character and

good record, his despair over the loss of his job, and the fact that he was no threat to public safety.

3. It violated the principle of proportionality, that the punishment should not exceed the gravity of the offense.

4. The crimes to which the mandatory law applied were arbitrarily selected and bore no rational relationship to public safety, dangerousness, culpability, law enforcement, or deterrence of crime.

Michael had made one stupid mistake, the hold-up. He was truly contrite and, in my judgment, did not need "rehabilitation," assuming that prison would provide such treatment. The prosecutor appealed the sentence.

Michael served his six months. After release, with the help of his probation officer, he obtained a job and repaid the $50.

Four years later the Supreme Court of Pennsylvania ordered me to resentence Michael to five years in the penitentiary. The fact that he had been law-abiding and working steadily supporting his wife and child since his release was considered irrelevant. The statute mandated a five-year prison sentence.

Faced with the choice of violating a court order or imposing a sentence that I believed was contrary to long-established principles of justice and fairness, I left the bench.

The judge to whom Michael's case was reassigned was also dismayed. He imposed the required five-year sentence but permitted Michael to remain at liberty on nominal bail in order to appeal to the Supreme Court. Probably realizing the futility of attempting to reargue the issue, Michael quietly disappeared. In 1993, he still had not been found. He has not been arrested. But if he should be involved in a traffic accident, apply for a job that requires a police check, apply for credit, or be involved in one of many other countless legal acts, the ubiquitous computer will ferret out his past and he will have to serve five years in prison and probably extra time for absconding. . . .

A Rage to Punish

A national survey in 1988 disclosed that 68 percent of the population believes that the country has lost ground in the area of crime. But the response has been more punitive laws and longer prison sentences, as well as judicial decisions restricting judicial discretion and the right of prisoners to appeal these harsh penalties.

These laws have taken a particularly heavy toll on the poor, who are most often imprisoned. They are also most frequently the victims of crime. Because non-whites, women, and children are disproportionately poor, the criminal justice system is weighted against them, not only in the pattern of arrests and the trial of cases but especially in sentencing. These are the unintended consequences of the rage to punish.

After the civil disorders in the 1960s, the Kerner Commission issued a report with this ominous prediction:

> To continue present policies is to make permanent the division of our country into two societies: one largely Negro and poor, located in the central cities; the other largely white and affluent, located in the suburbs and outlying areas.

This warning was not heeded. Instead, sentencing laws have exacerbated racial hostilities and have widened the gulf between the affluent and the poor. We are now a nation divided between *them*, the prisoners who are largely poor and non-white, and *us*, who are not incarcerated and who are largely white and non-poor.

Instead of addressing the causes of the civil disorders, a plea for law and order during the late 1970s was powerfully appealing to the American public. Legislators were motivated to "do something" about crime. "Soft judges" were a ready target. The old philosophy of rehabilitating felons was deemed to have failed.

A different rationale was needed. The doctrine of "just deserts" was appealing. Exactly what a felon "deserves" as punishment for his or her offense was never articulated. It was assumed to be either a long period of imprisonment or the death penalty.

With little discussion and no empirical evidence as to the effect the application of this theory would have on the public, the offenders and their families, the courts, and the prisons, legislators embraced the new dogma.

In 1971, when I was appointed to the bench, judges had discretion to impose sentences they deemed appropriate so long as the penalty did not exceed the statutory maximum. This had been the practice in the United States and in England for generations. At that time the death penalty had fallen into disuse in America, and in 1972 it was declared unconstitutional by the United States Supreme Court.

A Crime Control System

Mandatory sentencing laws and guideline sentencing laws enacted in the late 1970s and 1980s have transmogrified the criminal law from a justice system to a crime control system. The theory was that if a potential law violator knew that the penalty was a long prison sentence fixed by statute, individuals would be deterred from committing crimes. Discretion in imposing sentence was removed from the judge in order to eliminate perceived disparities in sentences. All offenders guilty of the same crime would receive the same penalty, regardless of race, sex, age, or mental condition.

It soon became evident that these laws drastically increased

144

the numbers of prisoners and the length of prison sentences. They also exacerbated the disparities in treatment between the affluent and the indigent, women and men, whites and non-whites, young offenders and older persons.

Dictating Justice

Congress created a Sentencing Commission in 1984 to establish sentencing guidelines for all crimes. Two years later, Congress blatantly ignored the commission and decided that only Congress could be trusted to determine the appropriate sentences for drug offenders. What followed was a congressional betting war to see which members could be toughest. Much like a poker game, members of Congress upped the ante until drug sentences exceeded those for most other crimes. As one congressman later noted, if someone had suggested the death penalty, another member would have tried to top it.

. . . Mandatory sentences undermine a traditional principle of justice in this country—that the punishment should fit the crime. These mandatory sentences, based solely on the type of drug and its weight, have left justice out of the equation altogether. Usually trusted to give an appropriate sentence to each defendant, judges are forced in federal drug cases to rely on a chart and deliver the disproportionate sentences that Congress has dictated. The legislators who in effect impose the sentence never meet the defendant and know nothing about his case, background, or likelihood of rehabilitation.

Julie Stewart, *Reason*, April 1993.

Congress enacted more than sixty laws mandating long prison sentences; every state then adopted one or more mandatory sentencing laws. Congress also adopted sentencing guidelines, as did approximately one-third of the states. And after the United States Supreme Court upheld the constitutionality of the death penalty in 1976, thirty-six states enacted death penalty statutes.

These laws were drafted and adopted with good intentions. The legislatures wanted to "control crime." They wanted to stop the bloodbath of murders. And they wanted offenders to be sentenced equally and fairly. These good intentions have not been realized. Crime has not been materially reduced. Homicides continue on the streets, in the schools, and in the homes. The discrimination against non-whites, women, children, the poor, and the mentally ill has been exacerbated. And the prisons have been filled to overflowing. The results have been disastrous to offenders and their families and to the taxpayers.

From the 1920s to the early 1970s, the rate of incarceration in the United States was stable at approximately 110 prisoners for every 100,000 residents. By 1986, it was more than 200 per 100,000 residents. It is higher today. The average length of prison sentences has also drastically increased during these two decades. In England, the length of all sentences is much shorter and the crime rate much lower. . . .

All Crimes Are Not Equal

In the United States, the goal of "equal justice under law" is generally assumed to mean that similarly situated persons should be treated similarly when they commit the same acts. But all crimes, despite the nomenclature—robbery, arson, assault, etc.—are not the same. And neither are all offenders who commit these acts. One thief may be a clever, well-educated, mature man who steals via computer. Another may be a functionally illiterate youth who snatches a pair of designer sunglasses. One killer may be a man who in cold blood stabs to death a cheating associate. Another may be a beaten wife or girlfriend who stabs to death her abuser.

Today, sentencing laws in the United States mandate penalties that are on the face of it non-discriminatory, but that in operation are race-, gender-, youth-, and ignorance-biased, laws that ignore individual differences under the rubric of neutrality and equal treatment. Thoughtful, concerned judges question the justice of the laws they are sworn to uphold and enforce.

Professor H.L.A. Hart, a learned British jurist, dismisses the qualifications of a judge to participate in such a discussion. He writes: "No one expects judges or statesmen occupied in the business of sending people to the gallows or prison, or in making (or unmaking) laws which enable this to be done, to have much time for philosophical discussion of the principles which make it morally tolerable to do these things."

This statement betrays, I believe, a misunderstanding of the role of the judge. We judges are not in a business. We are duly elected or appointed public officials, charged by the public with awesome responsibilities. Our function is not sending people to the gallows or prison but to adjudicate, based on the facts and the law, and to impose just and proper penalties on the guilty. It is true that we have little time for abstract discussion. But, as moral persons, we are deeply concerned with the justice and fairness of what the law requires of us. And trial judges are far better situated than any other professionals to see the often tragic consequences of the decisions the law impels.

"Some insist that civil forfeiture unfairly imposes on 'innocent owners.' Nonsense! Only the morally culpable have their property at risk."

Civil Forfeiture Is Fair

Bruce Fein

Civil forfeiture laws allow the government to seize property used during the commission of a crime if the noncriminal owners knew or were willfully blind to the fact that the property was being used for criminal activity. Some critics have argued that these laws are unfair because they penalize noncriminals. In the following viewpoint, Bruce Fein argues that civil forfeiture is fair because only those owners who ignore the unlawful use of their property are at risk of having it seized. Community involvement is an essential requirement in the fight against crime, he contends, and forcing owners to be aware of how their property is being used is not unreasonable. Fein is a lawyer who frequently writes about legal issues.

As you read, consider the following questions:

1. How does an owner get his or her seized property back from the government, according to Fein?
2. Why are some of the charges against civil forfeiture invalid, in the author's opinion?
3. Why does the author argue against indigent owners' receiving free counsel to get their property back?

Bruce Fein, "Taking a Look at Civil Forfeiture," *Washington Times*, August 24, 1993. Reprinted by permission of the author.

Clamors to curb civil forfeiture laws are swelling. Terrance G. Reed, an American Bar Association civil forfeiture adviser to the National Conference of Commissioners on Uniform State Laws, has charged: "[Forfeiture laws have] become a Kafkaesque nightmare for some property owners, who have found themselves caught up in a world of bizarre legal doctrine, sometimes without assets even to defend themselves."

Rep. Henry Hyde, Illinois Republican, and American Civil Liberties Union president Nadine Strossen, ordinarily philosophical antipodes, have jointly championed a civil forfeiture reform bill. And John Conyers, Michigan Democrat, chairman of the House Government Operations Committee, has voiced support for an even greater overhaul of forfeiture laws.

With but one exception concerning the government's burden of proof in civil forfeiture, however, no relaxation is justified. It is an important law enforcement tool, and the obligations it places on ordinary citizens to prevent use of their property to assist crime are not unreasonable.

Confiscations and Fairness

Civil forfeiture statutes seek a type of ostracism or boycott of those involved in a criminal enterprise. Generally speaking, they expose property used to commit crimes to forfeiture if noncriminal owners knew of or were willfully blind to that exploitation. Property is subject to government seizure by proof of "probable cause" to believe its use in crime. To prevail against the government, a property owner must prove by a preponderance of the evidence either the absence of crime, knowledge or willful blindness.

The U.S. Supreme Court ruled in June 1993 in *Austin vs. United States* that the Eighth Amendment prohibition on "excessive fines" requires that the magnitude of a forfeiture bear some reasonable relationship to the seriousness of the wrongdoing. The Austin decision further hinted that civil forfeiture would be unconstitutional absent proof of owner culpability. The Supreme Court acknowledged in *Caler-Toledo vs. Pearson Yacht Leasing Co.* (1974): "To the extent that . . . forfeiture provisions are applied to [those] innocent of any wrongdoing, confiscation may have the desirable effect of inducing them to exercise greater care in transferring possession of their property."

Civil forfeitures have been assailed because they can be triggered without criminal convictions, and lack criminal justice procedural safeguards, for example, jury trial or cross-examination rights. But in many cases, perpetrators of crime escape apprehension. The protective features of criminal justice—such as exclusionary rules or Miranda strictures on interrogation—may thwart justice. Thus, fairness is unaffronted by declining to make convictions a precondition of civil forfeiture.

The latter proceedings justifiably omit criminal justice safeguards because the owner whose property is at stake risks no criminal punishment or stigma. Concededly, the forfeiture of property serves a deterrent or punitive purpose. But the same can be said of civil treble damage statutes in federal antitrust and securities laws and punitive damages in tort litigation; yet the defendants in such cases are bereft of criminal justice safeguards.

Incriminating Evidence

Advocates of civil forfeiture like to point out that 80 percent of those who have property taken don't contest the seizures. "In the bulk of our cases, the circumstances are so incriminating that nobody wants to challenge us," Cary Copeland says. [Copeland is the director of the Justice Department's Office for Asset Forfeiture.] "With all that crime out there, we don't have to run around and take property from innocent people."

David A. Kaplan, *Newsweek*, January 4, 1993.

Some insist that civil forfeiture unfairly imposes on "innocent owners." Nonsense! Only the morally culpable have their property at risk—that is, those who knew or were willfully blind to its commandeering for criminal use. The law occasionally imposes criminal punishment and frequently creates liability for lesser or no culpability.

Criminal Conduct

In *United States vs. Park* (1975), the Supreme Court concluded that federal food and drug laws fasten criminal liability on corporate executives who fail to seek out and remedy violations or decline to implement measures that will ensure violations not occur. In other words, the absence of foresight and vigilance in forestalling violations of law can be made criminal itself.

It is commonplace in tort law to extract damages from defendants who unreasonably failed to anticipate criminal conduct. For instance, if a hotel owner neglects to provide adequate security to protect patrons from rape or robbery, persons injured by such crimes because of the negligence are entitled to damages. The owner's innocence of crime is no defense.

Strict tort liability, a fixture of contemporary law, requires defendants to pay damages without proof of morally censurable conduct. An imperfect car design, for example, can result in massive liability.

Mr. Hyde and Miss Strossen are correct in animadverting

against the low "probable cause" standard that justifies civil forfeiture. In criminal law, persons may be arrested and detained pending trial based on probable cause of complicity in crime. But a final judgment of punishment requires proof of guilt beyond a reasonable doubt. It seems blatantly unfair to authorize the government to forfeit property if it is unable to prove by a preponderance of the evidence its use in crime. That standard is the norm for civil plaintiffs, and there seems no reason to bend the norm to advantage the government.

Mr. Hyde and Miss Strossen would demand the government to win its case by "clear and convincing evidence," and to provide attorneys for indigents. But such deviations from ordinary civil litigation are unwarranted. The social interest in quarantining property from criminal activity is greater than that in deterring negligence. Vindication of the former thus should not be made more difficult.

In numerous civil suits initiated by government, small business or individual defendants decline to resist because of the costs of litigation. They do not receive free counsel. Why should persons allegedly culpable in permitting use of their property in crime receive more indulgent treatment?

Civil forfeiture laws correctly teach that community involvement is instrumental to criminal deterrence. Insisting that citizens exercise reasonable alertness over their property to avoid assisting crime is not asking too much.

"The guilt or innocence of the property owner is of no relevance in determining the outcome of the civil forfeiture case."

Civil Forfeiture Is Unfair

John Perna

Civil forfeiture statutes allow the government to seize property it suspects was used in the commission of a crime. In the following viewpoint, John Perna charges that because of these laws, many innocent people have their money and property seized for no reason other than the color of their skin or for being in the wrong place at the wrong time. The laws are unfair, he maintains, because even when the owners are innocent of any crime, their property is presumed guilty until proven innocent. Even when innocent owners are vindicated, Perna asserts, they often do not recover their entire loss. Perna is a contributing writer for the *New American*, a publication of the John Birch Society.

As you read, consider the following questions:

1. Why do prosecutors have an obvious advantage in civil forfeiture cases, in Perna's opinion?
2. What percentage of property seized belongs to people who have never been charged with a crime, according to the author?
3. What example does Perna use to show that every American is at risk of civil forfeiture laws?

John Perna, "Forfeiting Freedom," *New American*, May 17, 1993. Reprinted with permission.

In April 1989 deputies from Jefferson Davis Parish in Louisiana took $23,000 away from Johnny Sotello, a Mexican-American whose truck had overheated on the highway. They also seized his truck. Sotello was a licensed buyer with numerous auctioneer receipts to prove that his business was trading at heavy equipment auctions. But the police suspected another, more sinister explanation for the cash that Sotello was carrying: They had removed a door panel from Sotello's truck and found a space that they said could have been used to hide drugs. No drugs, however, were found. After two years of expensive legal battles, Sotello settled for the return of his truck and half of his money. The police kept $11,500, even though Sotello was never charged with a crime.

Willie Jones is a nursery man from Nashville, Tennessee. When he has enough capital, he visits Houston to buy shrubs. Out-of-town checks are not popular there, so he brings cash. On one such occasion, after having bought his airline ticket with cash, the ticketing agent reported the transaction to the police as being suspect. What was suspicious? Willie Jones was black, had money, and was on his way to Houston—a known "source" city for drugs. Police "pruned" Willie Jones of $9,600, even though he was never charged with a crime. He was told that in order to get his money back, he had to post a "bond" of an additional $900.

Dick Kaster is a fisherman with a story about the "one that got away" like no other fisherman has ever told. Unfortunately, Kaster's story is true. The Iowa Department of Natural Resources charged Kaster with having caught three fish with a gill net, a misdemeanor in Iowa. Their evidence was that these fish had "net marks." Kaster says that most of the fish had "net marks" and that he caught the fish with a rod.

The state of Iowa made the biggest catch of the day. Officers netted Kaster's boat, motor, and trailer. Even though this quarry was worth only about $6,000, the state spent another $100,000 defending the seizure. Kaster spent enough to restock several lakes. There is definitely something very fishy going on in America.

Aiding and Abetting Criminal Activity

That fishy something is enforcement of America's civil forfeiture laws in general and the 1984 Comprehensive Forfeiture Act (CFA) in particular. Civil forfeiture is a legal seizure which operates "in rem," meaning "against the thing." The guilt or innocence of the property owner is of no relevance in determining the outcome of the civil forfeiture case. The legal theory operates upon the fictional premise that the property itself has committed a crime. These kinds of cases give prosecutors an obvious advantage, since the property has no rights.

Under civil forfeiture laws, your car, boat, or house can literally be charged with the crime of aiding and abetting a criminal activity. As owner of the property, you may also be charged with a crime and placed under arrest, but this is not necessary for the forfeiture laws to be applied.

A Law Run Wild

Civil asset forfeiture, once viewed as a good way to make drug lords pay for their own arrests, prosecutions and incarcerations, has slipped from its leash. Programs to recover assets associated with crime appear to be victimizing the innocent. . . .

Horror stories abound of innocent people caught up in the forfeiture programs now used extensively by federal, state and local authorities. . . .

A 61-year-old California rancher was shot dead during the confusion of an early morning raid of his 200-acre property in a fruitless search for marijuana. A later investigation by the district attorney's office concluded there never was marijuana being cultivated on the property and the raid was motivated in part by a "desire to seize and forfeit the ranch."

Henry J. Reske, *ABA Journal*, October 1993.

Since 1989, the federal government has seized more than $2.2 billion in "forfeited" assets. About 80 percent of the property seized is lost by people who are never even charged with a crime. One reason civil forfeitures have increased dramatically is that the 1984 act allows law enforcement agencies to keep what they seize. Even informants are allowed to keep a portion of what is seized.

In civil forfeiture cases, the government is able to turn on its head the principle of "innocent until proven guilty" by making itself the new legal owner of the property. Lawsuits in which persons are trying to win the return of their property become civil rather than criminal matters. The "former" owner then bears the burden of proof in court as a plaintiff would in any other civil matter. In other words, the seized property is considered guilty until proven innocent.

Who Is at Risk?

Although many Americans mistakenly believe that no one is affected by government seizure programs except "drug kingpins," everyone is at risk. An example of how civil forfeiture laws can affect law-abiding citizens is the case of Ethyl Hylton. Miss Hylton left New York City, planning to buy a house in a warmer climate. She carried her entire life savings with her, which she had accumulated after working 20 years as a hotel housekeeper and a hospital janitor. Together with a recent $18,000 insurance settlement, she had over $39,000.

Upon her arrival in Houston, a Drug Enforcement Administration (DEA) agent told Miss Hylton that she was under arrest because a drug dog had scratched at her baggage. Her baggage and purse were searched, and Miss Hylton herself was even strip-searched, only to discover that she had no drugs. The DEA cleaned it all up by taking all but $10 of her life savings, even though Miss Hylton was never charged with a crime.

If you think that a "mistake" of this magnitude could never happen to you, think again. Dr. Jay Poupko of Toxicology Consultants Inc. in Miami, Florida tested U.S. currency from major cities for over a seven-year period. He found that 96 percent of the bills in his study tested positive for cocaine. Even the "drug contaminated" bills that are seized by the government are simply deposited in the bank. One of these could be among those that you withdraw to buy your next plane ticket.

The Burden of Proof

One hallmark of the American judicial system has been the requirement that the "burden of proof" must be borne by those making an accusation. Under the law, the accused should always be considered "innocent until proven guilty." All seizures should be subject to the ultimate criminal conviction of the owner of the forfeited property. Seizures made against individuals in cases where there is insufficient evidence to convict ought to have their property returned along with civil restitution in the amount of their attorney fees. Forfeiture should be defined as part of the punishment, with the requirement that the punishment must fit the crime, not the financial portfolio of the accused.

"America's criminal justice system is tilted decidedly in favor of the criminal as opposed to the victim."

Victims Should Be Involved in Criminal Trials

Joseph Perkins

Crime victims are not adequately represented at criminal trials, charges Joseph Perkins in the following viewpoint. In most states, he maintains, the rights of the accused are scrupulously upheld while victims are largely excluded from the courtroom. He argues that the balance is changing, however, as more and more states adopt victims' rights laws, which give victims the right to be present and heard at every stage of a criminal trial. Perkins is an editorial writer for the *San Diego Union-Tribune*.

As you read, consider the following questions:

1. Why are victims excluded from criminal trials, according to Perkins?
2. Why does an imbalance exist between victims' and criminals' rights, in the author's view?
3. What solution does Perkins support to give crime victims more rights?

Joseph Perkins, "Victims' Rights Rising," *Washington Times*, November 12, 1992. Reprinted by permission of the author.

The victims' rights movement continues to gain momentum. On Election Day in 1992, voters in Illinois, Missouri, Kansas, Colorado and New Mexico approved amendments to their constitutions that accord victims of crimes the right to be both present and heard during court proceedings.

This guarantee seems almost incidental. Many of us assume that the interests of victims are adequately represented in criminal trials. But nothing could be further from the truth. America's criminal justice system is tilted decidedly in favor of the criminal as opposed to the victim.

When a criminal case enters the system, the government supplants the victim, who becomes little more than a witness and has no legal standing. Victims are frequently excluded from courtroom proceedings, and prosecutors are under no legal obligation to consult with them before striking a plea-bargain agreement.

"I wasn't at the hearing. I wasn't at the sentencing," says Betty Jane Spencer, who survived a mass murder attempt that claimed the lives of her four sons. After the horrible tragedy at her rural Indiana home that was further aggravated by her indifferent treatment by the criminal justice system, Mrs. Spencer helped establish the Protect the Innocent Victims Advocate Foundation.

Mrs. Spencer still sees much injustice in the way victims and their families are treated. She notes that, even with the progress of the victims' rights movement over the past decade, the families of victims normally are not attending trials. That is because defense attorneys contrive legalistic excuses to exclude victims or their families, she says.

The reason that defense attorneys can get away with, well, murder, is that in all but a handful of states victims' rights are covered by statutory rather than constitutional law.

Thus, in states without constitutional amendments, victims have no recourse if pertinent laws are not followed to the letter. Meanwhile, the rights of criminals are scrupulously observed throughout the judicial process.

This imbalance owes, in large part, to our constitutional tradition. The Founding Fathers thought it important to provide certain protections for those charged with criminal offenses. Thus, five of the first 10 amendments to the U.S. Constitution have to do with the rights of the accused.

An Amendment for the Victim?

When the Founders ratified the Bill of Rights, they hardly could have imagined that, two centuries later, one of every eight citizens of the Republic would be victimized by crime year by year. Or that more Americans would be murdered in a given year than were slain by the Redcoats during the entire Revolutionary War. Had they foreseen this, they very well might have included at least one amendment setting forth the rights of victims.

Maybe it is time that the modern Congress do what the Founding Fathers neglected to do: Balance the constitutional rights of crime victims with those of the accused.

How Americans Feel About Victims' Rights

A majority of Americans consider victims' rights "very important," such as notification about trials and permission to attend them, according to an April 1991 National Victim Center survey. Respondents also supported victims' right to be alerted about the release of criminals, to receive compensation and to present impact statements in court.

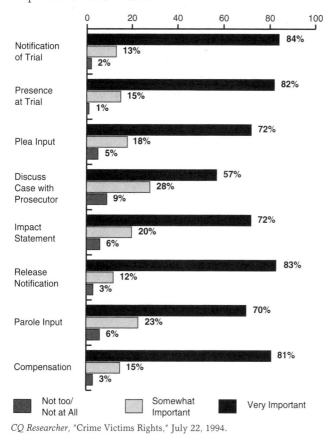

CQ Researcher, "Crime Victims Rights," July 22, 1994.

The simplest way to strike this balance is to modify the Sixth Amendment. This amendment, which addresses the judicial process, specifies the right of the accused to counsel, to an impartial jury and to confront witnesses. A sentence could be added at the end of the Sixth, declaring that the victim in every criminal prosecution shall have the right to be present and to be heard at all critical stages of judicial proceedings.

This was the language suggested a decade ago by a presidential task force on crime victims. Its proposal to amend the federal Constitution did not get very far then, but with the growing strength of the victims' rights movement throughout the country, perhaps at last such an amendment can get a hearing in Congress.

As to those who look askance at any proposed constitutional changes, they might consider the words of Thomas Jefferson: "I am not an advocate for frequent changes in laws and constitutions, but laws and institutions must go hand in hand with the progress of the human mind."

It certainly would be progress to give America's 35 million crime victims the same standing under the law that is now enjoyed by criminal offenders. A constitutional amendment affording basic victims' rights is the way to make this happen.

"Yelling epithets in a courtroom may indeed be therapeutic for victims, but personal therapy is not a defensible purpose of criminal trials."

Victim Impact Statements Are Prejudicial in Trials

Jeffrey Rosen

Victim impact statements, in which crime victims tell the court how they have been affected by the crime against them, do not have a place in the courtroom, argues Jeffrey Rosen in the following viewpoint. These statements inflame judges and juries, he maintains, and often contain irrelevant or prejudicial evidence. He concludes that a victim's rage should play little role in the determination of a criminal's proper punishment. Rosen is a senior editor for the *New Republic* magazine.

As you read, consider the following questions:

1. Why were victim impact statements excluded from death penalty trials prior to 1991, according to Rosen?
2. When the Supreme Court reversed its ruling about victim impact statements, what evidence was and was not allowed, according to the author?
3. How should judges and juries decide cases and sentences, in Rosen's view?

Jeffrey Rosen, "Victim Justice," *New Republic*, April 17, 1995. Reprinted by permission of the *New Republic*; ©1995, The New Republic, Inc.

> I know I have an impossible request, your honor. But given five minutes alone with Colin Ferguson, this coward would know the meaning of suffering. . . . [To Ferguson]: Look at these eyes. You can't look at 'em, right? You can't. You remember these eyes. You're nothing but a piece of garbage. You're a [expletive] animal. Five minutes. That's all I need with you. Five minutes.
>
> —Robert Giugliano, who was shot by Colin Ferguson

The anguish of the victims at the trial of Colin Ferguson was deeply moving, and their statements have been applauded as the only redeeming feature of an otherwise ghoulish spectacle. [Ferguson was convicted in early 1995 of killing six commuters and wounding nineteen others on New York's Long Island Rail Road in December 1993.] "If death was in that Long Island courtroom, so was life—affirmed by speakers who were in one way or another Mr. Ferguson's victims," the *New York Times* concluded. "[T]he participation of victims at the post-conviction stage is a healthy development," agreed the *Washington Post*. "It provides a catharsis for the surviving victim or his family, allowing those who have suffered to be heard."

We beg to differ. Of course, victims of crimes should have opportunities to find catharsis for their pain. But the dispassionate forum of public sentencing should not be one of them. Since Congress passed the Victim and Witness Protection Act of 1982, at least thirty-six states have allowed victim impact statements at trials. Most states require the statements to be written by a probation officer or state official, who can give an objective assessment of the harm caused by the crime. A few states, though, such as California and New York, allow the victims to speak at sentencing. This innovation has been widely criticized as a recipe for inflaming judges and juries with raw emotionalism. The Ferguson trial illustrates that the criticisms have been understated.

Yelling epithets in a courtroom may indeed be therapeutic for victims, but personal therapy is not a defensible purpose of criminal trials, which are conducted in the name of the people at large. Before 1991, the Supreme Court excluded evidence of the suffering of a victim's family in death penalty trials on the grounds that the character of the victim is irrelevant to the defendant's blameworthiness, especially since many murderers know nothing about their anonymous victims. In *Payne v. Tennessee*, the Court reversed itself and upheld the use of victim impact statements in capital cases. But seven justices took care to distinguish legitimate victim impact evidence, such as evidence about the character and suffering of the victim and survivors, from irrelevant and prejudicial evidence, such as the survivors' personal opinions about the defendant and the sentence he or she deserves.

The circus in Long Island shows the impossibility of filtering out legitimate from prejudicial evidence when victims are encouraged to voice their unmediated rage. Several of Ferguson's victims called on the judge to impose the maximum sentence. ("Dear honor, may you put him away forever in prison. No parole. Ever.") One even called for the death penalty, which was not yet available in New York. ("I believe it is within the moral rights of this society to sentence Colin Ferguson to death. . . . May God have mercy on you and this court have none.") The judge later told the survivors that he was profoundly moved by their anger, which is precisely what judges are not supposed to be moved by.

Do Not Punish Because of Suffering

Under the current state of the law, the victim has the greatest power at the stage where he or she least deserves and needs it—at sentencing. As a structural matter, the system can tolerate victim input at the time of sentencing, for at that stage everything is admissible. Everyone in town has a say about what should be done with a convicted felon. The victim too might as well fuel the public's lust for vengeance or promote the virtue of forgiveness. It would be a mistake, however, to privilege this input from the victim and treat it as critical to a proper level of punishment.

Punishment responds to the wrong the offender commits, but not to the particular wrong as measured by victims willing to testify. Killing a homeless beggar is as great a wrong as depriving a family of a loved one. Or at least that is what we have always assumed about homicide. It hardly makes sense to think of life as sacred if its value is a function of how much others love or need the person killed. That the victim is a human being is sufficient to determine the evil of killing. Thus the suffering of the survivors hardly seems the right basis for determining, say, whether the death penalty is justified.

George P. Fletcher, *With Justice for Some*, 1995.

The most basic requirement of the rule of law is that judges and juries must be personally impartial, that they can't decide even close cases on the basis of their sympathy or distaste for one party or another. Yet victim impact statements, when presented orally without the possibility of rational evaluation, guarantee that trials will degenerate into lawless emotionalism. As George Fletcher of Columbia Law School argues in *With Justice for Some*, the pain suffered by victims, which is highly relevant in determining the proper compensation in a personal injury case, should play little role in determining the proper punishment in a criminal case.

The celebration of emotionalism in criminal trials is part of a broader, Oprah-esque trend in public life, whose creed, as Yale law professor Paul Gewirtz argues, is "I feel, therefore I may judge." But criminal trials are designed to resist the talk-show creed. Judges and juries, unlike television viewers and victims, must decide guilt on the basis of reason rather than emotion, and punishment on the basis of public values rather than private rage. Perhaps the liberal state can't be saved from the hydraulic pressure of emotionalism. But a liberal legal system cannot survive it.

Periodical Bibliography

The following articles have been selected to supplement the diverse views presented in this chapter. Addresses are provided for periodicals not indexed in the *Readers' Guide to Periodical Literature*, the *Alternative Press Index*, or the *Social Sciences Index*.

Doug Bandow	"California's Three Strikes Law Strikes Out," *Wall Street Journal*, April 19, 1995.
Peter Cassidy	"Without Due Process," *Progressive*, August 1993.
CQ Researcher	"Mandatory Sentencing," May 26, 1995. Available from 1414 22nd St. NW, Washington, DC 20037.
Daniel Franklin	"The Right Three Strikes," *Washington Monthly*, September 1994.
Edward Grimsley	"Living Up to the Promise of Equal Justice," *Conservative Chronicle*, May 3, 1995. Available from PO Box 29, Hampton, IA 50441.
David A. Kaplan, Bob Cohn, and Karen Springen	"Where the Innocent Lose," *Newsweek*, January 4, 1993.
Stephen Labaton	"Cash-Poor Defendants May Soon Lack Lawyers," *New York Times*, August 9, 1992.
Patrick A. Langan	"No Racism in the Justice System," *Public Interest*, Fall 1994.
Edwin Meese III	"Three-Strikes Laws Punish and Protect," *Insight*, May 16, 1994. Available from 3600 New York Ave. NE, Washington, DC 20002.
Richard Miniter	"Ill-Gotten Gains," *Reason*, August/September 1993.
Carol Moseley-Braun and Laura Murphey Lee	"Symposium: Juvenile Justice," *ABA Journal*, March 1994. Available from 750 N. Lake Shore Dr., Chicago, IL 60611.
Stephen Reinhardt	"The Trickle Down of Judicial Racism," *Harper's*, August 1992.
Julie Stewart	"Establish Justice," *Reason*, April 1993.
Franklin E. Zimring	"Tough Crime Laws Are False Promises," *Insight*, May 16, 1994.

How Do the Media Affect the Legal System?

The
Legal
System

Chapter Preface

When Karla Homolka was tried for manslaughter by the Ontario Court General Division in July 1993, the judge in her case, Francis Kovacs, imposed a restriction on the media, prohibiting them from publishing or broadcasting her plea bargain agreement or any of the legal evidence or details of the case until after her estranged husband, Paul Bernardo, was tried, an event that did not take place until two years later. Kovacs wanted to ensure that the jury pool for Bernardo's trial was not contaminated by the evidence from Homolka's trial. "The considerations for a fair trial outweigh the right to freedom of the press in these exceptional circumstances," Kovacs wrote when announcing his decision. Kovacs was not the only Canadian judge to restrict the media during trials. Almost 60 judges imposed media restrictions during trials in 1993.

Such an action would be unheard-of in the United States. Although two of the rights guaranteed by the Bill of Rights—freedom of speech and the right to an impartial jury—seem to be in conflict with each other, many people believe they can coexist without compromising justice. Richard Stack, an assistant professor of communications at the American University in Washington, D.C., and a former public defender, argues that "'unaware' is not synonymous with 'impartial,'" nor is an impartial juror guaranteed by the Sixth Amendment. High profile cases often experience media saturation, but Stack contends that a juror can hold an opinion about the defendant's guilt or innocence and still render a verdict based on the evidence presented at the trial. Trying to empanel a jury that knows nothing about the case being tried is not only a waste of time, Stack contends, but irrelevant.

Numerous studies refute Stack's assertions of juror impartiality, however. Gary Moran and Brian L. Cutler found in two separate cases that as the amount of negative pretrial publicity increases, the defendant's perceived culpability in the eyes of the potential jurors increases as well. Despite the fact that 80 percent of these prospective jurors still believe that they can be impartial, Moran and Cutler maintain that the jurors' assertions of impartiality are implausible. They contend that a potential juror's claim of impartiality is more a response to "social desirability pressure" than the ability to put the news accounts out of their minds.

Must jurors be ignorant of a case in order to be impartial? The effect of excessive pretrial publicity on a jury's impartiality is just one of the topics the authors debate in the following chapter on the media and the legal system.

"In a technological age, cameras in the courtroom are no more than the manifestation of the right to observe the proceedings."

Televising Trials Is a Public Right

Anna Quindlen and Eileen Libby

In Part I of the following two-part viewpoint, nationally syndicated columnist Anna Quindlen argues that televised trials extend the public's right to attend a trial. Sensationalistic trials have always drawn a crowd, she contends, and televising the proceedings allows more people to make up their own minds about the evidence. In Part II, Chicago attorney Eileen Libby asserts that watchers of the cable channel Court TV learn about the judicial process and know whether a defendant received a fair trial or if a sentence was justified. Although Court TV broadcasts trials involving crimes of sex and violence to attract viewers, it also provides educational legal programming, she maintains.

As you read, consider the following questions:

1. Why does Quindlen discount the theory that televising O.J. Simpson's trial would prevent him from receiving a fair trial?
2. What are the benefits of televising trials, in Quindlen's opinion?
3. Why is Court TV more like C-Span than *Matlock*, according to Libby?

I

Some years ago I stood behind a teacher with a gaggle of students who had approached a court officer at the Criminal Courts Building in lower Manhattan to ask how she could arrange to observe a trial. The officer told her what he later said many people failed to understand: that anyone can watch.

It's that simple: the public usually has a right to be present at the process by which we find our fellows guilty or not of some infraction of law. Today, as the O.J. Simpson case has made clearer than ever before, we even have the right to watch from the comfort of our living rooms.

Despite an orgy of hand-wringing about prurient interest and pretrial publicity, nothing in this case, no non-existent ski mask, no car chase, not even the damning and surely inadmissible 911 tape of Nicole Simpson begging for help as her enraged ex bellows in the background, has been as compelling as the preliminary hearing and the public scrutiny it has inspired.

Those who watched the proceedings, televised in their entirety day after day, listened to a slow accretion of circumstantial evidence: the sales clerk who sold a knife, the limo driver who got no answer at the house, the police officer who found blood on the driveway.

Some viewers found the argument of police that they had scaled the wall of the defendant's house because of their fear of an emergency compelling; others thought it was a flimsy excuse to circumvent a search warrant.

Ordinary people argued about the testimony, just as someday jurors may do the same. They learned about the Fourth Amendment and the tedium of trial procedure. "It was a tremendous civics lesson," said Jeanine Pirro, the Westchester County, N.Y., district attorney.

It's important not to forget that it was the defense, in what was clearly a monumental miscalculation, who solicited this wholesale exposure.

The hypothesis was that the preliminary hearing would force the prosecution to show its hand; the reality is that much damaging evidence became public knowledge to millions of viewers.

But the notion that all this forecloses Simpson's ability to get a fair trial is a simplistic reaction to a complex process.

Countless small towns have seen trials in which evidence, gossip and innuendo were bruited about across every back fence. Jury pools have been culled in big cities after publicity almost as widespread—and as erroneous and irrelevant—as that in this case.

Publicity and the Trial

Certainly great publicity may make the process more onerous. In the so-called "preppy murder" case [in which Robert Chambers, 19, strangled Jennifer Levin, 18, during sex in Central Park in New York City, in 1986], it took a pool of nearly 500 New York citizens to come up with 12 jurors and four alternates.

The prosecutor, Linda Fairstein, used a peremptory challenge to remove one potential juror, a young woman who felt moved to tell the defendant, Robert Chambers, that he was even better looking in person than in his pictures.

Television as Society's Mirror

Televising court cases does not distort the administration of justice; it portrays it for what it is: tedious at times, dramatic other times, sometimes formal, but always human. If we don't like what we see on court television—primping participants, the vagaries of the adversary system, the perversity of the jury system, the way rich folks get better treatment than others—isn't it simplistic to complain that television is the cause? The trashy, inflammatory and prejudicial coverage of the O.J. Simpson case has not been in the gavel-to-gavel television but in all the commentary about it.

I believe we are better off seeing trials than not, warts and all, and that if any reform is ever to come from any perceived flaws in "the system," it will only come after public exposure. History proves that the more government operates in the open, the better.

Throughout the history of the "public trial" requirement of the common law, the rationale has been to demonstrate the workings of the judicial system to the people, and to discourage perjury and encourage witnesses to come forward. . . .

Television is society's mirror; like Howard Cosell, it "tells it like it is." Presently, the judicial system is the only part of our government that resists the openness of television. The public has much to learn from what goes on in our courts, in civil and criminal trials, and even in the more cerebral appellate courts. The Supreme Court's public work, for example, would provide a rare and valuable civics lesson if it could be widely viewed. Who would be hurt?

Televising trials can be an edifying and self-righting practice. "We must judge television as we find it," the late Justice John Harlan stated, and I agree. But in judging, we must be careful that it is the medium we are judging and not its message, or messengers.

Ronald Goldfarb, *American Journalism Review*, December 1995.

The tut-tutters complained then and complain now that the public is interested in following only the most salacious of cases. (The tut-tutters always talk about the public as though it were a large hairy animal with poor hygiene and eating habits.)

So what? While viewers may tune in because O.J. Simpson is famous and the murders of Nicole Simpson and Ronald Goldman savage, they may stay to learn about suppression of evidence.

While opponents of cameras in the courtroom have insisted that such scrutiny could intimidate witnesses and lead lawyers to grandstand—imagine that! lawyers grandstanding!—it's just as possible that all involved may instead be on their best behavior in the camera's unforgiving eye.

And while there is great concern about tabloid shows and newspapers that pay for interviews, the truth is that this atmosphere may make the press better at what it does.

Full coverage of courtroom proceedings allows viewers to make their own decisions about the high points, the sound bites, the good quotes and to be properly critical of the synthesis they see on the evening news and in the newspapers.

But whether any or all of these things follow from the up-close scrutiny of this or any other case is in some measure irrelevant. As the court officer told the teacher, anyone can come inside.

In a technological age, cameras in the courtroom are no more than the manifestation of the right to observe the proceedings.

In the case of the People vs. Simpson, the people have shown up in force.

II

Okay, I confess. I'm one of those Court TV junkies who was glued to the tube by the daily sagas of Lyle and Erik [Menendez, who killed their parents in 1989] and Lorena [Bobbitt, who cut off her husband's penis with a kitchen knife in 1993]. My mail piled up, my phone calls went unanswered, but I didn't care. Lyle Menendez' impeccable hairpiece and lousy upbringing, [his defense attorney] Leslie Abramson's courtroom histrionics, Lorena Bobbitt's unhappy homelife all became major events in my life.

But that doesn't make Court TV an exercise in tabloid television. Its "gavel-to-gavel" coverage of trials includes not just neat, gut-wrenching moments but messy stretches of delays and boring, often poorly organized presentations of evidence. It doesn't matter much if a trial is lurid and sensational—Court TV is capable of reducing it to real-time tedium. In short, Court TV is closer in spirit to C-Span than to *Matlock*.

This is not a bad thing, however. Court TV is designed to offer viewers an opportunity to talk back to the set. It invites informed opinion and discussion by exposing the judicial process, warts and all. Court TV anchors are teamed with knowledgeable color commentators to explain the key plays in the game. There is also continuing legal education programming during off-hours and a weekly wrap-up of legal news from Washington.

Unlike the viewer whose only source of information about the law is the nightly news or the op-ed pages, the Court TV viewer knows with greater certainty whether a defendant was fairly tried or whether a lenient sentence was justified. And anyone who listens to Court TV's nightly call-in segment knows that its audience is not made up of voyeuristic Beavis-and-Butthead clones looking for cheap thrills, but of informed citizens who know the difference between rebuttal and redirect.

For this educational process to occur, however, the viewer's attention must be wrested away from competing cable channels, network television and video games like "Mortal Kombat." Any self-respecting channel surfer is unlikely to bypass *Oprah* or *Melrose Place* to watch a televised antitrust or trademark infringement trial.

All-American Entertainment

Like a carnival barker who lures the public into the tent with glimpses of flesh, Court TV often must appeal to baser human instincts. For old-fashioned, all-American entertainment, nothing beats the real thing: That's why trials about patricide, sexual mutilation or baby buying draw the largest numbers.

Fortunately, the educational function goes on regardless of a case's subject matter. Every trial makes demands of jurors and of the viewing audience. And each one is a set piece of argument, character development and explanation. There are experts to expound new theories, strategic maneuvers, and flashes of excellence and mediocrity.

For example, the Court TV audience was shown all of [defense attorney] Roy Black's masterful cross-examination of Patricia Bowman in the 1991 William Kennedy Smith rape trial, a privilege now enjoyed by a few criminal law classes on video. Trials drawn from today's headlines can rivet our attention long enough for us to learn what courtroom buffs have known all along—that real-life trial drama can be more compelling than the fictionalized version.

The Menendez boys and Lorena Bobbitt may be the stuff of made-for-television movies, but there is a great deal to be learned from listening to their stories, whole and unfiltered. We wouldn't be debating the validity of the so-called victimization defense if Court TV hadn't thrown it in our faces every day for six months, live and in living color. In a perfect world, Court TV might be more dignified, but it couldn't do a better job of bringing the law to life.

"If O.J. Simpson has a constitutional right not to testify before 12 jurors, why expose him to the unrelenting scrutiny of 120 million?"

Televising Trials Demeans Justice

Max Frankel

Television cameras in courtrooms should not enjoy the same First Amendment protections as the written press, contends Max Frankel in the following viewpoint. Viewers of televised courtroom proceedings may judge the defendant's guilt based on such criteria as superficial facial expressions, he argues, and not on the evidence. Trials should not be televised without the consent of all parties involved, he maintains. Frankel is a columnist with the *New York Times Magazine*.

As you read, consider the following questions:

1. What are some of the arguments for allowing cameras in the courtroom, according to Frankel?
2. How are televised trials different from written accounts of trials, in the author's view?

All my working life, my pencil, pen, typewriter or laptop has shared my protection under the First Amendment. ("Congress shall make no law . . . abridging the freedom . . . of the press.") Where I went, my tools went—as a matter of right and law. So I came to believe that the rights enjoyed by my writing implements logically belonged also to television cameras. They also serve reporters and, sad to say, they bring news to more people than all newspapers combined. Although the Founding Fathers failed to anticipate TV news anchors Peter Jennings, Tom Brokaw and Dan Rather, the TV cameras, like my pencils, seemed to qualify as evolutionary descendants of Ben Franklin's quill.

No longer. After watching the O.J. Simpson [who was charged with the murder of his ex-wife and her friend] hearings with morbid fascination, I have a new sense of relationships: my pencil is to a television camera as Judge Ito's courtroom is to Titus's Colosseum.

A Different Beast

I don't say ban cameras from all trials. Nor do I blame the camera inside the Simpson courtroom for *all* the scandalous coverage, tawdry gossip and misinformation swirling around this case. But I am certain now that the camera is not just another incarnation of "press," entitled to the unabridged freedom thereof. It's a different beast that should enter a court by a different door, under different rules.

That is not a popular opinion among news people. Conflict is our favorite kind of news and a life-and-death trial our favorite kind of conflict. Most television producers surely believe, now that they can't show Roman gladiators in mortal combat, that making do with the verbal jousts of defense attorney Robert Shapiro and prosecutor Marcia Clark is concession enough to modern sensibility.

The champions of the camera rightly observe that it has become unobtrusive; it no longer needs hot lights or flashing bulbs like those that disrupted the trial of the Lindbergh baby kidnapper. The fear that witnesses would feel intimidated by the camera has been largely dispelled in the 47 states that admit it to criminal courts. The fear that cameras would provoke some lawyers to ham up the proceedings is surely misplaced; they normally need no provocation and if they do the cameras on the courthouse steps would suffice.

So open up, say the networks, especially Court TV, the cable channel that offers round-the-clock coverage and analysis of the most telegenic cases. It made its mark with sensations, notably the trials of William Kennedy Smith [acquitted of rape in 1991], Lorena Bobbitt [not guilty by reason of temporary insanity of the malicious wounding of her husband in 1993], Lyle and Erik

Menendez [charged with killing their parents in 1989] and the cops who beat Rodney King [in 1991]. But it argues now that it is the antidote to sensationalism: "With the circus atmosphere surrounding trials today, cameras inside the court are needed more than ever."

Cameras as Proxy

Most newspapers support that opinion. The *New York Times* recently editorialized that while television viewers may at first be attracted by a defendant's celebrity or a murder's savagery, "they may stay to learn about suppression of evidence." Come for kicks, stay to be taught. In any case, the *Times* and others contend, "cameras in the courtroom are no more than the manifestation of the right to observe the proceedings." We can't all fit, so the camera carries our proxy for the right to attend. Constitutional lawyers keep trying to settle the matter by stretching the First Amendment around television cameras, but the Federal courts resist, leaving state courts and legislatures to respond in their fashion.

Reprinted by permission of Dale Stephanos/*Boston Herald.*

I've spent many an evening with Court TV and much prefer it to the fake trials of "L.A. Law" or "Law and Order." And then came Simpson. Wow! I could stare into O.J.'s eyes for a hint of remorse. I could read Shapiro's face for a clue to his faith in his client. I could study Marcia Clark, head to toe, wondering how the football crowd would react to No. 32 being prosecuted by this woman. I couldn't stop watching.

But neither could I stop resenting the voyeur in me. Sorry, *New York Times*, I was not just learning the laws of search and seizure. I was rushing to judgment about the honesty of the police and of the lawyers, the fairness of the judge and, yes, the guilt of the defendant—not on the evidence . . . but by the looks of things, by the flick of an eye, the twist of a lip, the jut of a jaw.

And sitting in judgment with me, I realized, were millions of other jurors. Like our forebears in the Colosseum, we were turning thumbs up or down on the performers even before the trial had really started. As always in a big case, the frenzied leaks and lies about the evidence made matters worse. But it's the camera that is transforming our involvement with justice. Prose accounts of the same proceeding beg to be analyzed; live pictures are consumed. Words on paper or from talking heads are easily recognized as secondhand; they even whisper "beware of the messenger." Images on a screen draw us into the action; they pound the emotions, bypass the mind.

Scrutinized by 120 Million People

If O.J. Simpson has a constitutional right not to testify before 12 jurors, why expose him to the unrelenting scrutiny of 120 million? To sit for weeks and months before a multitude that devours every frown, smile and tear is a punishment before judgment, a trial as practiced in old Rome, a crucible so fierce that it ought to offend us no less than a televised hanging. And while the noise level may be lower when there's no celebrity on screen, the notoriety that the camera confers can scar any defendant for life. Reporters and spectators must attend trials to guard against a star chamber proceeding. But no camera should come into court without the defendant's consent.

I would let a prosecutor and judge object as well. Though there is no proof that television coverage alters the conduct of a case, the suspicion that it does inevitably grows as the camera magnifies the din and compounds the stakes, in fame and fortune, for every participant. Justice may not often be compromised but society's sense of it can certainly be demeaned.

"For the powerless in our culture who knowingly open themselves up to very personal stories that should be told . . . it seems only fair that they should be compensated."

Checkbook Journalism Helps Achieve Justice

Louise Mengelkoch

In the following viewpoint, Louise Mengelkoch asserts that checkbook journalism—in which victims, assailants, or witnesses sell their story to the media—is sometimes the only way an injured party can achieve justice. The tabloids may be tawdry, but by focusing attention on those who are not fairly treated by the legal system, Mengelkoch contends, they may help justice to be served. It is only fair to sources that they be financially compensated for exposing their private lives to the media, she maintains. Mengelkoch teaches journalism at Bemidji State University in Minnesota and is writing a book about the incident described in this viewpoint.

As you read, consider the following questions:

1. Why did the county prosecutor urge the Lorys not to discuss the case with the media, according to the author?
2. What, other than money, were some of the benefits the Lorys received for selling their story to the media, in Mengelkoch's view?
3. In the author's opinion, what is the tabloids' greatest virtue, and why?

Louise Mengelkoch, "When Checkbook Journalism Does God's Work," *Columbia Journalism Review*, November/December 1994. Reprinted by permission.

It seems that at least once a day I read something in the popular press about the shameful nature of the tabloids and, especially, tabloid television. "Checkbook journalism" has become the buzzword for the unsavory practice of paying Michael Jackson's personal servants, or Bill Clinton's bodyguards, or the store clerk who sold O.J. Simpson a knife to tell all, whether it's true or not.

Money taints the truth, we reason. And the stories themselves appeal to the lowest common denominator in terms of subject matter, audience, and focus. Having said that, I'd like to tell about a strange tabloid story in which I became involved.

A Small-Town Rape and Murder

I spent a year immersing myself in reporting a rape and murder story. During that year, I changed my thinking drastically about the value of sensationalism and checkbook journalism. Specifically, I now think we, as journalists, and the public would be better served by re-educating ourselves about what the television tabloids are good for, and why.

In August 1993, fourteen-year-old Heather Lory was gang-raped in the wee hours of the morning by three boys, two of them brothers, in a country cemetery near my home in rural northern Minnesota. Later that morning her parents, Richard and Linda Lory, drove to the boys' home to confront them and their family. Richard Lory ended up shooting seventeen-year-old Bruce Bradach Jr., one of the three boys, to death, seriously wounding Bruce Bradach Sr., and accidentally shooting his own wife in the stomach.

I read the account of the incident in our local newspaper, *The Pioneer* of Bemidji, which was based entirely on official sources: the police report, the complaint, the county attorney. It was obviously superficial and incomplete and that was because of circumstances at the 9,000-circulation daily that I was well aware of; many of my students go on to work there. This is a newspaper that requires its reporters to write an average of seven stories a day (of varying length) and pays reporters little more than minimum wage.

A week later, the *St. Paul Pioneer Press* featured a front-page article on the case, even though we're a long 250 miles northwest of the Twin Cities. This time, the story was based on official sources plus eyewitness accounts by unofficial sources. But more confusion was created by a different kind of resource-allocation problem. The big-city reporter's time was too valuable to spend more than a day or so in the woods of Nowhere, Minnesota. So he interviewed the people who were willing and available: the Bradach family, friends of theirs, a woman who worked with Rich Lory's wife, Linda, and Rich Lory's former employer. Linda Lory was recovering from surgery and was too ill to speak, and the reporter was told by jail administrators that Lory would not grant an interview. What the reporter didn't know was that the county attorney had instructed everyone involved to stay away from the media, and Lory was not even told about the reporter. The Bradachs ignored the instructions and, as a result, were at least able to speak their piece. The Lorys felt they'd been had, especially when the county attorney himself was quoted at length.

Making the Facts Fit

Among his off-the-cuff remarks was the assertion that Bruce Bradach Jr., the young man killed, had nothing to do with the rape. (He apparently based that statement solely on the Bradach family's story. Much later, DNA testing strongly suggested otherwise; final DNA testing was never done.) After the article appeared, Heather Lory was called a liar, a slut, and a murderer more times than she could count. She was spit upon at football games, received death threats, sometimes on her assignment notebooks. She finally dropped out of school.

For the people in our community, the St. Paul paper's article solidified a few basic "facts" around which everything else now had to fit. When I read it, I was puzzled and intrigued enough to contact the Lorys and ask for an interview. I wanted to hear their side of the story, I said, and perhaps write a commentary for a Twin Cities paper.

They grabbed onto my offer with more hope than I was comfortable with. The Lorys later said they had gone to the Bemidji paper to tell their side, but were rebuffed. The reasons given were the negative side effects of pretrial publicity and the need to "protect" Heather's privacy. The Lorys even approached the campus newspaper of the state university at which I teach. The family reasoned, quite rightly I thought, that the story was relevant to our campus because Rich Lory had just graduated summa cum laude that spring with a degree in elementary education, to add to his degree in psychology from some years ago. The *Northern Student* editors didn't know quite how to handle the situation and gave the Lorys mixed messages about their willingness to print their story.

My position was clear—I thought. I would hear their side, interview the Bradach family, and write a short opinion piece decrying twin evils: the timidity of the small-town, corporate-owned press—in this case, the owner was Park Newspapers of Ithaca, New York—in the face of controversy, and the big-city's bumbling parachute journalism. I'd shake hands with all involved and go back to my classroom. It wasn't quite that simple.

The Bradach family had now decided to heed the advice of

the county attorney and gave me only one brief, unsatisfying interview. The official sources now mysteriously took the high road and wouldn't discuss either the rape or the killing. The Lory family wanted to talk but were being consumed by several imminent disasters: Linda and the four children were, day by day, fast losing their hold on economic sufficiency. She had lost her job, her car had been repossessed, Rich's phone calls from jail were costing an average of $150 a month, and the Minnesota fall was fast turning to winter with no money for fuel oil.

Sharing the Benefits

Even when they do pay for stories, tabloid producers insist, the practice is used carefully and does not compromise credibility. *Inside Edition* anchor Bill O'Reilly argues that paying for interviews is a legitimate way of competing with the networks, whose offer of prime-time national exposure carries more clout. "To level the playing field, we have to offer incentives to some people to come on our air." Some journalistic watchdogs agree that the traditional stigma against pay-for-play reporting may be breaking down—and for good reason. "It's hard to argue that the ordinary person shouldn't share in the benefit of what's going to be a commercial product," says Everette Dennis, executive director of Columbia University's Freedom Forum Media Studies Center.

Jeffrey Ressner, *Time*, December 6, 1993.

Rich Lory was warm and well-fed but lived in a bleak prison of ignorance about his own case, which, he said, was worse than the actual jail. He had a court-appointed lawyer with whom he'd met only once. The public defender's message was simple—be prepared to spend a long, long time in prison because your case seems pretty open and shut and I'm busy. See you in six months or so. We'll get together about a week before your trial begins. (Lory was also led to believe that pretrial publicity could be damaging to his case and could even cause a change of venue.)

Getting the Story Told

Watching all this go on with my reporter's notebook in hand, I was reminded of photographers documenting acts of violence or horror they could stop if they'd put down the camera. I couldn't stand it. And yet, at the same time, I was beginning to see a larger, long-term story here that I wanted for myself. I worried that if I published part of the story now, I would cut off future sources in opposing camps. When I expressed this concern to

178

my husband, who is also a writer, he agreed, and said he would write a commentary himself.

He entitled it "Is Justice Blind? Or Is it Deaf and Dumb in Rural Minnesota?" The *Star Tribune* in Minneapolis wasn't interested, but the *St. Paul Pioneer Press* took notice. They didn't print it, but the editorial page editor called us. We explained the situation, and he passed my husband's piece to the reporter who'd written the original front-page story, who then called us. He said he knew he should have pushed harder to get a wider variety of sources and wondered if we thought that Lory would agree to be interviewed at this late date. I said it was probably worth a try. He came up.

When Linda Lory asked my advice about granting the interview, I cast aside all pretense of being the disinterested chronicler of events. I warned her that it wouldn't be their story as told through the reporter. It would be his story, and they would undoubtedly be very unhappy with some aspects of it. Furthermore, they would have no way of correcting any new misperceptions the new article caused. The Lorys decided that any publicity that might help find an acceptable lawyer for Rich and clear Heather's name in the community was worth the risk.

The reporter came up and spent several days doing long interviews with the Lorys and re-interviewing the Bradachs and official sources after reading hundreds of pages of transcripts at night in his motel room. He wrote a thoughtful article, focusing on Heather's ordeal, but also mentioning the problems faced by Rich Lory. The Lorys did dislike aspects of the story. But they tried to focus on the long-term good it could do. They were hoping for a break.

The Big Break

It came soon after the story ran in late November 1993. A producer for the *Sally Jessy Raphael* show was visiting her family in St. Paul for Thanksgiving and saw the article. The Twin Cities local television news reporters called. Linda Lory was excited but fearful and uncertain. Rich Lory was impatient and suspicious. Dealing with reporters so intense they wanted to land helicopters on the Lorys' front yard or producers so insensitive they didn't realize the Lorys couldn't afford a long-distance phone call proved to be too much for the family. So my husband and I ended up brokering with the TV producers and reporters for the Lorys.

The *Sally Jessy* show came first, in early December 1993. We negotiated for some extras, beyond all travel expenses, for the Lorys: paid child care for their younger children while Linda and Heather traveled to New York; expenses for the student reporter who had ultimately written the Lorys' story for the campus newspaper; partial expenses for me; and a guarantee that the Bradach family would not appear on the stage with them.

There were some annoying problems. We felt patronized and pressured during the entire experience. Heather was in tears over the inappropriate clothes—too grown-up and sophisticated—the producers tried to make her wear on stage. Linda Lory was told to pay her expenses for later reimbursement when she was so broke she couldn't have afforded up front money to tip the limo driver.

Legitimizing Their Concerns

But the show, broadcast in January 1994, was an unqualified success for the Lory family. They had an hour of air time to tell their story to more than six million viewers. Until then they'd assumed that somehow they were responsible for the system's not working, for Heather's harassment, for Rich Lory's frustration. But the professionals who appeared with them on the show and those in the audience reassured them. And the TV appearance gave them a sense of authority in our own community and legitimized their concerns and complaints. Now it was up to the local powers to respond.

The powers that be were furious. In a front-page story in the local paper, the county attorney vilified the family for their decision to appear on national television and congratulated himself and the Bradach family for taking the high road and refusing to appear. All in all, the town was in an uproar.

After that, things happened fast. *Hard Copy* and *American Journal* wanted the story. We went with *Hard Copy*, the one willing to pay the family $3,000, what the Lorys felt they needed as start-up money to get a lawyer for Rich. That $3,000, and the videotapes of TV appearances, did result—by March 1994, one month before the scheduled murder trial—in a lawyer who agreed to work for expenses only. The lawyer gave the family renewed purpose.

At his trial, Rich Lory was found not guilty of first-degree assault on Bruce Bradach Sr. and not guilty of second-degree murder. He was found guilty of felony murder, a lesser charge in Minnesota. But before sentencing, improprieties of the jury's deliberations were discovered, and a new trial was ordered. The case has been highly scrutinized locally and statewide ever since the national media paid attention.

After the trial, the Lory family, the Bradach family and the defense attorney all appeared together on the Phil Donahue show to tell their stories, the Bradachs by remote hookup from their home, Rich Lory by phone from jail. I was invited to come to offer my observations as well. The entire Donahue organization displayed nothing but the highest degree of professionalism in all our dealings with them. All involved came away feeling they'd had their say. Expenses were paid fully and promptly.

The reporter and producers of *Hard Copy*, as well, were extremely professional in their demeanor and in their editing. They took their time, asked probing and sensitive questions, and followed through on their promises.

Tabloids Care About Truth

There may not be much difference between the money the tabloid shows pay and the ego gratification that network magazine shows offer when they induce sources to appear on nationwide television with Diane Sawyer or Barbara Walters or Connie Chung. (Reporters who went to the home of the daughter of an O.J. Simpson juror after the trial were prevented from seeing her when an ABC producer said she had agreed to speak exclusively to Sawyer.)

But whether the appeal is money or vanity, producers and reporters on tabloid TV shows say the most important question about a news source is not why the source is speaking but whether the reporter believes the source is telling the truth, or embellishing it to attract the highest (or most glamorous) bidder.

David Shaw, *Los Angeles Times*, October 9, 1995.

The publicity has now died down. One of the Bradach boys, sixteen, and a thirteen-year-old whose mother has since married Bruce Bradach Sr. pleaded guilty to sexual misconduct and were sentenced as youthful offenders to probation and counseling. Rich Lory awaits his new trial, and his wife and children are trying to piece their lives together. [Lory was found guilty of felony murder in September 1995.] But the impact on those lives from their willingness to "sink" to the level of tabloid journalism has been nothing but positive.

Positive Changes

Linda Lory has been transformed from a woman too timid to speak to a news reporter to one who was able to put herself on the agenda of a county board meeting and make a public speech about her appearance on national television. Heather Lory has apparently found some healing in public discussion of her case and in support from other women and girls. She has said she hopes that other young women will gain the courage to confront their rapists and trade shame for openness. Rich Lory found a lawyer he probably never would have found otherwise and now faces a maximum of eight to twelve years instead of the forty years the public defender predicted. [Lory was sentenced to twelve and a half years in prison after his second trial in 1995.] All three Lorys get phone calls and letters of support. People comment on how grateful they are for the opportunity to try to understand how this happened and prevent it from occurring again.

Another benefit of the tabloid exposure that went beyond the Lory family was the light it shone on local public officials. This normally doesn't happen here. It became apparent as the case progressed that some irregularities had taken place and that such things were considered business as usual. Certain people and offices were so unused to public scrutiny that they trapped themselves over and over by forgetting how things should be done. The Lory trial got gavel-to-gavel coverage from the Minneapolis newspaper and a 2,000-word front-page story when it ended.

There is still the question of that $3,000 payment from *Hard Copy*. I understand all the arguments against checkbook journalism. It's hard not to see the potential abuse and the bizarre extremes to which potential sources will go. But for the powerless in our culture who knowingly open themselves up to very personal stories that should be told—that have a real message for the public—it seems only fair that they should be compensated for their willingness to go public. My only complaint is that the Lorys didn't get more.

This experience has educated me in another way too: I use it in my teaching. I bring into class all the normally private people in our county I can find who've been in the news: the young mother whose ex-husband has been charged with abducting their three-year-old daughter; the woman whose grandson accidentally shot and killed his brother; the student in our class who was shot in her backyard while having a barbecue. We discuss the attention they've gotten, talk about how people like them should handle the media and what they can hope to accomplish from the attention. We talk about how to choose someone to handle the media for you or how to approach a friend you can see is having trouble handling the media and offer to help. And, yes, we talk about the tabloids and whether negotiating with them would be a wise option in each case.

The Tabloids' Greatest Virtue

The tabloids' greatest virtue, I tell my students, is exactly what makes people sneer at them—they're often foolish and not very selective. As gatekeepers they're lousy, and that's often fortunate for those who need them most. They will listen to your story when nobody else will, if it has the elements they're looking for. If we truly believe in access, that journalists should be dedicated to comforting the afflicted and afflicting the comfortable, the tabloids must be recognized as sharing that mission.

"Witnesses who take money from tabloids automatically raise questions about their credibility."

Checkbook Journalism Hinders Justice

Jeffrey Toobin

Sources who practice checkbook journalism—selling their stories to the media—seriously undermine their credibility in court, argues Jeffrey Toobin in the following viewpoint. When sources are paid for their stories, defense attorneys can easily cast doubt on whether these witnesses' testimony is truthful or simply what they were paid to say, he maintains. Toobin contends that witnesses and their agents may not realize that the loss of credibility they incur by receiving payments for their stories may ultimately result in a guilty person going free. Toobin is a reporter for the *New Yorker*.

As you read, consider the following questions:

1. How has checkbook journalism—witnesses' selling their stories to the media—affected the O.J. Simpson trial, according to the author?
2. To whom does the credit for "cash for trash," belong, in John Terenzio's view, as quoted by Toobin?
3. According to Raoul Felder, as quoted by Toobin, why is checkbook journalism okay?

Excerpted from "Cash for Trash" by Jeffrey Toobin, *New Yorker*, July 11, 1994. Reprinted with permission.

Robert Owens, an attorney from Los Angeles, had a cellular phone in one hand, a pen in the other, the sand of a Maui beach between his toes, and the riches of an O.J. Simpson–obsessed media on his mind. He represents Dale St. John, the owner of Town & Country Limousine, of Torrance, California, which is the company that sent a car to pick up the former football star and take him to the airport on what is now invariably referred to as "the fateful night" of June 12, 1994. "Obviously, Dale was one of the first people the police spoke to, and I know that what he said to them has not been published anywhere so far," Owens told me, over his phone, in a tone of shared intimacy. "Remember, Dale drove O.J. personally for several years, and he also had a lot of contact with the driver on the night of the murders. He hasn't made a deal with anyone yet, and he hasn't spoken to anyone yet, but he's at the point now where he's ready to make a deal with someone. That's why he called me."

The Costs of Checkbook Journalism

Owens symbolizes the state of the art in one of the newest specialties in the legal market—the brokering of interviews to the tabloid media. The cash-for-trash bar is not organized in any official sense—many of its practitioners dip in and out for just a single sale—but its influence is soaring in the prosecution of high-profile criminal cases. Because witnesses who take money from tabloids automatically raise questions about their credibility, and because defense attorneys can so successfully vilify those witnesses on cross-examination, the practice of buying and selling interviews seriously threatens prosecutors' abilities to try high-profile cases. Ironically, the print and television tabloids that fuel this industry have been widely denounced for their supposed rush to convict celebrity defendants before they have even been tried; as it happens, however, the tabloids can so taint the central witnesses in the government's case that tabloid infotainment may actually be the best friend a famous defendant can have. The torrent of press coverage of the Simpson case, tabloid and otherwise, cost the prosecution dearly. On June 24, 1994, Judge Cecil J. Mills, of California Superior Court, dismissed the grand jury investigating the case, because some jurors had been exposed to "potentially prejudicial matters not officially presented to them by the district attorney."

Certainly, it seems, the Los Angeles Police Department has come to recognize the costs of saturation coverage. This official acknowledgment came in a little-noticed coda to the first public announcement of the murder of Nicole Brown Simpson and her friend Ronald Goldman. After giving the basic facts about the case, such as the names of the victims and the place where the bodies were found, Commander David Gascon issued a plea to the news media. "Over the next few days, detectives will continue to interview possible witnesses, and gather and analyze evidence," Gascon said on June 13, 1994. "Detectives are requesting that the media not attempt to contact potential witnesses in this case, as those contacts may delay and negatively impact the course of this investigation. I need to stress that. It's critically important."

"WHO WOULD PROFIT FROM THIS BIZARRE MURDER? BESIDES TABLOID JOURNALISM, I MEAN."

Reprinted by permission: Tribune Media Services.

Steve Dunleavy, who is the lead correspondent for Fox television's "A Current Affair" and is also the Australian elder statesman of the tabloid industry, first heard about Gascon's request when I mentioned it to him, a few days later, in the course of a telephone call. "With all due respect to the L.A. police, they're a little Pollyanna when they ask reporters not to talk to witnesses," Dunleavy said. "We have an L.A. guy, and I'm just sort of tits on a reindeer out here, mate, but this is the story people are talking about, and we've got to be here." In fact, on the day that Dunleavy and I spoke, he had just interviewed Michael Mesko, a caddie at the Riviera Country Club, who had toted O.J. Simpson's bag around the course only hours before the murders took place. Mesko told Dunleavy that Simpson was alternately angry and maudlin during his round, and that at one point Simpson "turns to me and says, 'Mitch, I'm a pathetic person.'" Mesko added, "I was shocked." Dunleavy now chuckled, and said, "Nice little scoop for us. But, if that's how the police feel, best of luck to them, eh?"

Buying the Witnesses

Dunleavy's view also seems to be that of his colleagues in the tabloid press. "It's not just going to be witnesses in the case itself," one reporter for a supermarket tabloid told me. "Every woman O.J. went out with, every secretary, everyone who worked with him—they're all going to be hitting the money." Indeed, the buying of witnesses has already begun. A week after the murders, Paramount's television tabloid "Hard Copy" agreed to pay a potentially crucial witness named Jill Shively five thousand dollars for her recollections of the night of June 12, 1994. Holding up her grand-jury subpoena for the cameras, Shively said that she had seen a harried O.J. Simpson driving his Ford Bronco wildly near his home in Brentwood at about eleven o'clock. Adapting nicely to the overheated tabloid idiom, she declared that Simpson looked "like a madman gone mad, insane." At around the same time, the supermarket tabloid the *Star* paid Shively two thousand six hundred dollars for a print interview. And at the preliminary hearing in the Simpson case, two of the prosecution's opening witnesses revealed that they, too, had been paid for interviews with a tabloid. Allen Wattenberg, a co-owner of Ross Cutlery, the store where O.J. Simpson bought a knife shortly before the murders, and José Camacho, a salesman at the store, testified that they would be splitting a twelve-thousand-five-hundred-dollar payment from the *National Enquirer* with Allen's brother and partner, Richard.

Shively and the knife dealers sold themselves cheap. The *Enquirer* offered at least a hundred thousand dollars for an interview with Kato Kaelin, a family friend who was staying in the guesthouse at Simpson's estate on the night of the murders. "The guy from the *Enquirer* made it clear that the hundred thousand was negotiable," Kaelin's lawyer, William Genego, told me shortly after the offer was received. "He was clearly willing to go higher." Indeed, the *Enquirer* raised its offer to two hundred and fifty thousand dollars last week. But, Genego said, his client turned the offer down, along with all other interview requests, because "he didn't want to get into that whole distasteful business." Yet the tabloids expect to find no shortage of takers as they continue to offer money to witnesses in the Simpson case. "The thing of it is that the really big guns have not come up for bid yet," a tabloid editor told me ten days after the murders. "No one even knows the name yet of the limo driver. He'd be worth plenty. And the biggest money of all is for Al Cowlings"—Simpson's best friend, who was the driver in his nationally televised chase along the Los Angeles freeways. . . .

The Cash-for-Trash Industry

Credit (or blame) for the creation of the modern cash-for-trash industry belongs to the United States Supreme Court, according to John Terenzio, a former executive producer of "A Current Affair." "When they struck down the Son of Sam law, that's when everything started to change," he told me recently. The so-called Son of Sam law was passed by the New York State Legislature in 1977 to prevent David Berkowitz (who sent notes to the police signed "Son of Sam") from capitalizing on his notoriety as a serial killer. The measure made it illegal for criminals to earn income from selling stories about their misdeeds. In 1991, however, the Supreme Court ruled that the law violated the First Amendment. "Once that law was gone, we knew that the day would come when the Jeffrey Dahmers of the world would make a bundle," Terenzio said. "I wouldn't pay a convicted criminal, but it opened our eyes to what was out there—the deals to be made." The supermarket tabloids, led by the *Enquirer*, which has a weekly readership of nearly twenty million, have had no trouble keeping pace. I was told by David Perel, an editor at the *Enquirer*, "If someone has a great story to sell, and it can be exclusive for us, the price may be in the hundreds of thousands of dollars, and we're going to pay it.". . .

According to several tabloid executives, it was the Amy Fisher–Joey Buttafuoco affair in 1993 that first pushed prices into the stratosphere. A Fox check-authorization form that was provided to me showed that "A Current Affair" paid Buttafuoco five hundred thousand dollars for his cooperation. "The bottom line is that if you have a bad book"—that is, bad ratings during the sweeps period—"it can cost you millions of dollars in advertising," Terenzio explained. An executive at another television tabloid agreed. "The sweeps mean everything," this person said. "But not all the sweeps are the same. The November book is the most important, and, since our year starts in the fall, that's when we have the most money to spend on people. February is next, and by the time May sweeps come around we usually don't have much more money anyway. If you have a story to sell, November is the time you want to do it."

That the Michael Jackson child-abuse case exploded during the November sweeps is a source of everlasting dismay to Lauren Weis, who has been a deputy district attorney in Los Angeles for fifteen years and, as the head of the Sexual Crimes and Child Abuse Division, is leading the investigation of the singer for sexual abuse of children. By chance, she heard Commander Gascon's announcement of the Simpson murder, including his plea to the media to stay away from witnesses. "I certainly took note of what he said," she remarked to me recently. "I had never seen that before in a press statement by the police, but the times have changed. There's certainly been nothing before on the scale of what happened in my case."

Witness Credibility

In the light of her experience, Weis may have become the nation's foremost authority on the damage that the tabloids can inflict on a criminal investigation. "It's obvious that once witnesses have been paid a great deal of money their value as witnesses is lessened, in the sense that jurors will always wonder whether they're saying what they're saying because they were paid to say it," she said. "As a prosecutor, you can try to lessen the damage. You can say that they had already been interviewed by the police, and you hope to be able to show that once they were paid by the tabloids their story didn't vary. You can try to corroborate them with what other witnesses have said. But the damage is there." So incensed is Weis about the tabloids that she told me she was planning to propose legislation in California that would make the buying of interviews a crime in some cases. "I have actually been considering discussing some legislation where it would be illegal to pay a potential witness money to discuss a pending investigation. The law would say that when someone has reason to know there is a pending investigation that person can't be paid any money, so that the criminal prosecution would not be affected. I know that it would be challenged on First Amendment grounds, but I think that it would be upheld. I think it's worth it."

At present, as Weis's indignation makes clear, no legal or ethical rule bars lawyers from shopping their clients' stories from tabloid to tabloid. Deborah Rhode, a professor of law at Stanford Law School and the director of a legal-ethics center there, explained the situation by saying, "As the lawyer, your obligation would be to discuss the pros and cons with the client. You'd probably have to remind the client to balance the money he's getting against certain costs, such as long-term damage to his reputation. But it's true that it may be in both the lawyer's and the client's immediate interest to sell the story, especially if the lawyer's getting a percentage of the deal as a fee. The public has an interest in seeing the criminal process move ahead unimpeded, but the conventional answer is that we don't expect lawyers to suspend their obligations to the client out of broader societal concerns."

Aggressive Lawyers and the Media

As the prosecutors in the Simpson case set out to assess the threat that the tabloids will pose to the proceedings, they would do well to consider the example of Ted Mathews. He was one of their own—a former Los Angeles deputy district attorney in the sexual-assault unit. For that reason in particular, he is a special object of Lauren Weis's fury: she is now the head of Mathews' old unit. If, as many people expect, the Michael Jackson case ends without an indictment, Mathews may bear some responsibility for it. At the very least, Mathews' story is a sobering case study of the costs to society of the alliance between aggressive lawyers and the tabloid media. . . .

Fortune smiled on Mathews, in the form of the "Jackson five." Five former bodyguards at Michael Jackson's estate, in Encino, California, arrived on Mathews' doorstep bearing potentially lucrative troubles. The five men told Mathews, who by then was practicing with another lawyer, . . . that they believed they had been fired because they'd learned of their employer's pedophilia. Late on the afternoon of November 22, 1993, Mathews filed a lawsuit on their behalf against Jackson and several of his associates charging that the guards had been unjustly dismissed. When I visited Mathews, he still seemed to be savoring the reaction of the press to that move. "As soon as we filed, they were all over us like a cheap suit," he told me. . . .

"We started getting offers from lots of different places—the talk shows, the tabloid shows," Mathews went on. They kept asking me, 'How much did the others offer you?' I was totally amazed. One very sexy lady came to see me on behalf of one of the shows, and she never said so directly, but I got the sense that she would be—you know—available if that would help her show get an interview. As the money offers started coming in, I had to report them to my clients. They had been out of work for some time at that point, so they were interested." Because Mathews was representing the guards on a contingency-fee basis, he, too, stood to benefit from the proceeds of the sale of interviews. . . .

A Cash-for-Trash Alliance

On November 29, 1993, "Hard Copy" broadcast the first of three days' worth of Diane Dimond's highly rated interviews with the guards. Maury Povich also wrung a pair of shows from the guards' story, on December 13, 1993, and February 21, 1994. According to the guards' deposition testimony in their lawsuit against Jackson, each of the five received fifteen to seventeen thousand dollars, leaving Mathews with about twenty thousand as his commission. In our talk, Mathews declined to reveal his fee.

The interviews with the guards proved to be not just a one-shot deal but, rather, the beginning of a mutually beneficial relationship between "Hard Copy" and Ted Mathews—one that symbolizes the growing symbiosis between the tabloid press and the lawyers in the cash-for-trash bar. The aim of that alliance, of course, was money—for Mathews, for his clients, and, as the residue of high ratings, for "Hard Copy" and Paramount. How the buying and selling of witnesses' testimony might affect an active criminal investigation; whether crucial witnesses might be discredited by the fact that they auctioned their memories; how the assembled appetites might, in the end, help a serial pedophile escape punishment—these matters, it appears, never came up in the negotiations. . . .

Selling the Story

If Robert Shapiro and F. Lee Bailey, Simpson's current trial lawyers, ever face one of the witnesses who sold his or her story to the tabloids, they will have a useful script from the trial of William Kennedy Smith. The nephew of Senator Edward M. Kennedy was charged with raping Patricia Bowman at the family estate in Palm Beach. On December 3, 1991, toward the end of Smith's trial, Anne Mercer, a friend of Bowman's, took the stand to testify that Bowman had telephoned her for assistance from the Kennedy compound after the alleged assault. The prosecutor, Moira Lasch, sought to limit the damage to her witness's credibility by bringing out, during direct examination, how Mercer came to be interviewed by "A Current Affair."

"Why did you give an interview to 'Current Affair' concerning this information?" Lasch asked.

"I believed that my police statement was out already. I had already given four statements to the police, and I didn't feel that it would harm the case in any way," Mercer replied.

"Were you paid for those interviews by 'A Current Affair'?"

"I was compensated, yes."

"How much were you paid by 'A Current Affair'?"

"Twenty-five thousand for the first interview and fifteen thousand for the second interview."

People in the courtroom that day say they will never forget the reaction at that point. "There was this gasp—a really loud one—and it just went on and on," one of them recalled. "People were buzzing. The jury started talking. It was unbelievable.". . .

The American Way?

So what if she did make money, Raoul Felder [Mercer's lawyer] said to me. "She was able to make a sum. She didn't do anything illegal, immoral, or fattening. They offered her money and she took it." He shrugged. "It's the American way."

If that is true, then the American way has already cost the O.J. Simpson prosecution at least one witness. Jill Shively, the woman who saw a wild-eyed Simpson in his Bronco and then enjoyed the patronage of "Hard Copy" and the *Star*, might have proved to be a significant voice at the trial; her testimony casts doubt on Simpson's alibi that he was home by himself at the time of the murders. But the prosecutors in the case, Marcia Clark and David Conn, were aghast when they learned that Shively had sold her story. Shively was so shaken by Clark and Conn's reaction that she immediately hired her own attorney, James Epstein, who was summoned to an 8 A.M. meeting with the prosecutors on June 23, 1994. "They were absolutely furious," Epstein told me. "They said that they regarded Jill as an important witness, and she did testify in the grand jury, but they have decided not to use her anymore. Because she sold her story, they feel that the defense will be able to make it look like her testimony is false and that she only made it up to make money."

Periodical Bibliography

The following articles have been selected to supplement the diverse views presented in this chapter. Addresses are provided for periodicals not indexed in the *Readers' Guide to Periodical Literature*, the *Alternative Press Index*, or the *Social Sciences Index*.

George Bain	"The Criminal Trial as Sport Spectacle," *Maclean's*, February 20, 1995.
Massimo Calabresi	"Swaying the Home Jury," *Time*, January 10, 1994.
Erwin Chemerinsky	"Pretrial Publicity Isn't a Hindrance," *Los Angeles Times*, June 28, 1994. Available from Reprints, Los Angeles Times, Times Mirror Square, Los Angeles, CA 90053.
CQ Researcher	"Courts and the Media," September 23, 1994. Available from 1414 22nd St. NW, Washington, DC 20037.
Mark Curriden	"Tabloid Tales Hindering Prosecutions," *ABA Journal*, December 1994. Available from 750 N. Lake Shore Dr., Chicago, IL 60611.
Ronald Goldfarb	"The Wrong Villain," *American Journalism Review*, December 1995.
Myles Gordon	"Lights, Camera, Justice!" *Scholastic Update*, September 4, 1992.
Carole M. Gorney	"The Case Against Litigation Journalism," *USA Today*, March 1994.
Carole M. Gorney	"Fatal Attraction: Journalists and Lawyers," *Current*, July/August 1994.
Carole M. Gorney	"Litigation Journalism Is a Scourge," *New York Times*, February 15, 1993.
New Yorker	"He-e-ere's Justice," October 11, 1993.
Susanne Roschwalb	"Does Television Belong in the Courtroom?" *USA Today*, November 1994.
Jill Smolowe	"TV Cameras on Trial," *Time*, July 24, 1995.
Richard Stack	"The Impact of Mass Media on Jury Trials," *Champion*, September/October 1994. Available from 1627 K St. NW, 12th Fl., Washington, DC 20005.
Barry Tarlow	"Try It in Court, Not in the Press," *Los Angeles Times*, June 28, 1994.
Woody West	"Courtroom Cameras Are Guilty of Distorting American Justice," *Insight*, March 20, 1995. Available from 3600 New York Ave. NE, Washington, DC 20002.

Glossary

ABA American Bar Association.

ADR Alternative Dispute Resolution. A method of resolving a lawsuit through a mediator rather than through the courts.

American rule The custom in the United States wherein each party in a suit pays his or her own attorney's fees.

ATLA Association of Trial Lawyers of America.

attaint at common law The conviction of a jury for giving a false verdict, or a writ given after the conviction, reversing the jury's verdict.

change of venue Moving a trial from the city or county where the crime occurred to another location, usually because of excessive pretrial publicity.

civil law A legal system, found primarily in continental Europe and its former colonies, that is based upon statutes and legal codes.

common law The legal system used in England and the United States (excluding Louisiana, Puerto Rico, and the U.S. Virgin Islands, which use **civil law**). In common law, legal decisions are based on precedents set by past decisions.

contingency fee The fee a lawyer is awarded out of a **plaintiff**'s settlement. The fee is awarded only if the plaintiff wins the case.

comparative negligence How much more (or less) one is responsible than someone else for allowing something to happen.

contingency fee The fee a lawyer is awarded out of a **plaintiff's** settlement. The fee is awarded only if the plaintiff wins the case.

contributory negligence How much one's actions (or inactions) contributed to something happening.

defendant A person against whom a lawsuit or charge is filed in court.

de jure By right; according to the law.

discovery A process in which the **plaintiff** is given, either orally or in writing, necessary facts or documents held by the **defendant**.

English rule The system used in England in which the losing party of a lawsuit pays both parties' attorneys' fees.

equity case A case filed to stop some behavior of the **defendant** rather than for seeking monetary damages.

grand jury A jury made up of at least twelve persons whose sole function is to determine if enough evidence has been presented by the district attorney to warrant a trial.

jury nullification When a jury acquits a **defendant**, despite overwhelming evidence of guilt, because the jury believes the law or the application of the law to be unjust.

loser pays A form of the **English rule** in which the losing party of a lawsuit pays the opposing party's attorney's fees.

peremptory challenge The right to exclude potential jurors during jury selection without having to give a reason.

petit jury A jury usually made up of twelve, but sometimes six, jurors, who listen to the evidence in a trial and render a verdict.

plaintiff   The person or entity filing suit in court.

punitive damages   A fine against a **defendant** designed to punish "outrageous conduct" that has usually resulted in an injury.

substantive law   A law that creates and defines one's rights and responsibilities.

tort   A civil wrong or injury usually due to negligence.

voir dire   "To speak the truth." A process in which opposing lawyers question prospective jurors to search for evidence of bias.

writ   A legal document issued by a court that either orders something to be done or grants authority for the act.

For Further Discussion

Chapter 1

1. Chester James Antieau and the report from the Civil Justice Reform Task Force both agree that juries reach essentially the same verdicts as judges in civil trials, yet the authors use this point to support views that are diametrically opposed. What conclusion about juries does each author base on this observation? Which viewpoint do you agree with? Why?

2. Marcy Strauss argues that juror journalism—the media's practice of paying jurors for their accounts of a trial—is beneficial because it helps judges, lawyers, and the public better understand how juries reach their decisions. Abraham S. Goldstein contends that juror journalism thwarts justice because jurors, knowing their remarks may become public, are inhibited from freely discussing a case among themselves. Whose argument do you find more compelling? Why?

Chapter 2

1. Stephen Chapman maintains that a "loser pays" rule would discourage people from filing frivolous lawsuits, resulting in faster resolutions for those with meritorious lawsuits. John Conyers Jr. believes that a "loser pays" rule would deter many who have a reasonable claim from filing a lawsuit. Which viewpoint do you find more persuasive? Why?

2. Punitive damage awards are designed to punish wrongdoers for engaging in outrageous behavior. Sherman Joyce argues that awards for punitive damages should be capped at $250,000. Do you agree? Why or why not?

Chapter 3

1. R. Emmett Tyrrell Jr. places much of the blame for what he sees as America's litigation explosion on lawyers who use frivolous lawsuits as a scheme to get rich. Do you agree with his view of the American legal system and lawyers? Why or why not?

2. Glenn W. Bailey argues that unless tort laws are changed, many American businesses will not be able to compete with foreign corporations and will be forced out of business. Talbot D'Alemberte maintains that America's inability to compete is due to economic factors, not litigation. Whose argument is more convincing? Why? Does the fact that Bailey is the chief executive officer of a company that is facing

thousands of lawsuits influence your assessment of his viewpoint? Explain your answer.

Chapter 4

1. Alan Ellis contends that the criminal justice system discriminates against blacks, charging that perpetrators of crimes against blacks are treated more leniently than perpetrators of crimes against whites. Randall Kennedy contends that charges of discrimination in the criminal justice system are overblown and that aggressively prosecuting black criminals actually helps the black community. Whose argument do you find more convincing? Explain your answer.

2. Phil Gramm argues that mandatory minimum sentencing laws deter potential criminals from committing crimes. Lois G. Forer contends that judges should have the right to exercise their own discretion when sentencing criminals. Do you think mandatory minimum sentences are an effective deterrent? Support your answer with references from the viewpoints.

3. Bruce Fein maintains that criminal convictions should not be required before the government can confiscate property used during the commission of a crime. John Perna describes how he believes the government has abused its authority in civil forfeiture cases. Based on your reading of these viewpoints, do you think the property's owner should be convicted of a crime before the property can be confiscated? Why or why not?

Chapter 5

1. Anna Quindlen and Eileen Libby believe that television cameras in the courtroom benefit the public, while Max Frankel does not. What is your opinion? Support your answer with examples from the viewpoints.

2. Louise Mengelkoch describes how a family's selling their story to the tabloid media benefited the family involved. Jeffrey Toobin contends that witnesses who sell their stories to the media may be less believable in a courtroom. Does either author make a stronger argument about selling stories to the media? If so, why is it stronger?

Organizations to Contact

The editors have compiled the following list of organizations concerned with the issues debated in this book. The descriptions are derived from materials provided by the organizations. All have publications or information available for interested readers. The list was compiled on the date of publication of the present volume; names, addresses, fax numbers, and phone numbers may change. Be aware that many organizations take several weeks or longer to respond to inquiries, so allow as much time as possible.

American Bar Association (ABA)
Criminal Justice Section
740 15th St. NW
Washington, DC 20005
(202) 662-1500

Founded in 1920, the Criminal Justice Section of the ABA is an umbrella organization of over ten thousand members including prosecutors, private defense lawyers, law professors, public defenders, trial and appellate judges, law students, correctional and law enforcement personnel, and other criminal justice professionals. With its interdisciplinary membership base, the section takes primary responsibility for the ABA's work on solutions to issues involving crime, criminal law, and the administration of criminal and juvenile justice. Its publications include the quarterly *Criminal Justice* magazine and various reference books, course materials, and legal analyses.

American Tort Reform Association (ATRA)
1212 New York Ave. NW, Suite 515
Washington, DC 20005
(202) 682-1163
fax: (202) 682-1022

ATRA advocates changes in the current tort system to return fairness, efficiency, and predictability to the civil justice system. The association offers advocacy information and public education on legal issues. It publishes the semimonthly newsletter *Leaders' Update*, the weekly *Legislative Watch*, and the monthly newsletter the *Reformer*.

Brookings Institution
1775 Massachusetts Ave. NW
Washington, DC 20036
(202) 797-6000
fax: (202) 797-6004

Founded in 1927, the Brookings Institution is a liberal research
and educational organization that publishes material on economics, government, and foreign policy. It publishes analyses of
the legal system in its quarterly magazine the *Brookings Review*
and in its various books and reports.

Cato Institute
1000 Massachusetts Ave. NW
Washington, DC 20001
(202) 842-0200
fax: (202) 842-3490

The Cato Institute is a libertarian public policy research organization that advocates limited government and opposes most
mandatory minimum sentences that would force the early release of violent criminals. In addition to books and monographs
concerning the legal system, Cato also publishes the *Cato Journal* and the bimonthly *Cato Policy Report*.

Citizen Action Fund (CAF)
1730 Rhode Island Ave. NW, Suite 403
Washington, DC 20036
(202) 775-1580
fax: (202) 296-4054

The CAF works to make the concerns of the majority of Americans known in economic, environmental, and political decisionmaking. Its publications include the research report *The Verdict
Is In: Jury Awards Unchanged Over Thirty Years.*

Families Against Mandatory Minimums (FAMM)
1001 Pennsylvania Ave. NW, Suite 200S
Washington, DC 20005
(202) 457-5790
fax: (202) 457-8564

FAMM is an educational organization that works to repeal
mandatory minimum sentences. It provides legislators, the pub-

lic, and the media with information on and analyses of minimum-sentencing laws. FAMM publishes the quarterly newsletter *FAMM-gram*.

HALT: Americans for Legal Reform
1319 F St. NW, Suite 300
Washington, DC 20004
(202) 347-9600
fax: (202) 347-9606

HALT's goal is to reduce the cost of legal services and to find ways to expedite the litigation process. It believes that many cases can be settled with minimal or no lawyer intervention. Its publications include the monthly newsletter *Frontlines* and the quarterly magazine the *Legal Reformer*.

Heritage Foundation
214 Massachusetts Ave. NE
Washington, DC 20002
(202) 546-4400
fax: (202) 546-8328

The Heritage Foundation is a conservative public policy research institute. It is a proponent of limited government and advocates tougher sentences and the construction of more prisons. The foundation publishes articles on a variety of public policy issues in its *Backgrounder* series and in its quarterly journal *Policy Review*.

Justice Fellowship
PO Box 16069
Washington, DC 20041-6069
(703) 904-7312
fax: (703) 478-9679

The Justice Fellowship is a national criminal justice reform organization that advocates victims' rights, alternatives to prison, and community involvement in the criminal justice system. It aims to make the criminal justice system more consistent with biblical teachings on justice. It publishes the brochures *A Case for Alternatives to Prison*, *A Case for Prison Industries*, *A Case for Victims' Rights*, and *Beyond Crime and Punishment: Restorative Justice*, as well as the quarterly newsletter *Justice Report*.

National Association of Blacks in Criminal Justice (NABCJ)
North Carolina Central University
Criminal Justice Building, Room 106
PO Box 19788
Durham, NC 27707
(919) 683-1801
fax: (919) 683-1903

Founded in 1972, this organization is comprised of criminal justice professionals concerned with the impact of criminal justice policies and practices on the minority community. It seeks to increase the influence of blacks in the judicial system. Publications include the quarterly *NABCJ Newsletter* and the bimonthly *Local Criminal Justice Issues Newsletter*.

National Center for State Courts (NCSC)
PO Box 8798
Williamsburg, VA 23187-8798
(804) 253-2000
fax: (804) 220-0449

The NCSC acts as a clearinghouse for information on judicial improvement. It works to strengthen the structure and administration of trial and appellate courts, and it compiles statistics on state court caseloads and administrative operations. The center's publications include the monthly newsletter *Report* and the quarterly *State Court Journal*.

National Institute for Citizen Education in the Law (NICEL)
711 G St. SE
Washington, DC 20003
(202) 546-6644
fax: (202) 546-6649

The NICEL educates the public about issues concerning the legal system. It conducts student mock trials, teen action programs, and other law-related educational projects to promote knowledge and respect for the law. The institute publishes the semiannual *Street Law News* and various textbooks, articles, and brochures related to law.

National Institute of Justice (NIJ)
U.S. Department of Justice
PO Box 6000
Rockville, MD 20850
(800) 851-3420

The NIJ is a research and development agency that documents crime and its control. It publishes and distributes its information through the National Criminal Justice Reference Service, an international clearinghouse that provides information and research about criminal justice. Its publications include the bimonthly *National Institute of Justice Journal*.

The Roscoe Pound Foundation (RPF)
1050 31st St. NW
Washington, DC 20007
(202) 965-3500
fax: (202) 965-0355

The foundation works to strengthen the legal system by improving the trial bar and the jury system and by making the law more responsive to the needs of citizens. It publishes the book *The Courts: Separation of Powers* and the periodic *Papers of the Roscoe Pound Foundation*.

The Sentencing Project
918 F St. NW, Suite 501
Washington, DC 20004
(202) 628-0871

The Sentencing Project opposes mandatory sentences and works to develop alternative sentencing programs that would provide constructive options to incarceration. It publishes the reports *Americans Behind Bars: A Comparison of International Rates of Incarceration* and *Young Black Men and the Criminal Justice System: A Growing National Problem*.

Bibliography of Books

Jeffrey Abramson — *We, the Jury: The Jury System and the Ideal of Democracy*. New York: BasicBooks, 1994.

Stephen J. Adler — *The Jury: Trial and Error in the American Courtroom*. New York: Times Books, 1994.

David C. Anderson — *Crime and the Politics of Hysteria: How the Willie Horton Story Changed American Justice*. New York: Times Books, 1995.

Blanche Davis Blank — *The Not So Grand Jury: The Story of the Federal Grand Jury System*. Lanham, MD: University Press of America, 1993.

Robert H. Bork — *The Tempting of America: The Political Seduction of the Law*. New York: Free Press, 1990.

Citizen Action — "The Verdict Is In: Jury Awards Unchanged over Thirty Years." Report, Citizen Action, Washington, DC, 1995.

Frank M. Coffin — *On Appeal: Courts, Lawyering, and Judging*. New York: Norton, 1994.

Alan M. Dershowitz — *The Abuse Excuse: And Other Cop-outs, Sob Stories, and Evasions of Responsibility*. New York: Little, Brown, 1994.

Alan M. Dershowitz — *Contrary to Popular Opinion*. New York: Pharos Books, 1992.

Norbert Ehrenfreund and Lawrence Treat — *You're the Jury: Solve Twelve Real-Life Court Cases Along with the Juries Who Decided Them*. New York: Holt, 1992.

Stephen Elias et al., eds. — *Legal Breakdown: Forty Ways to Fix Our Legal System*. Berkeley, CA: Nolo Press, 1990.

George P. Fletcher — *With Justice for Some: Victims' Rights in Criminal Trials*. Reading, MA: Addison-Wesley, 1995.

Lois G. Forer — *A Rage to Punish: The Unintended Consequences of Mandatory Sentencing*. New York: Norton, 1994.

Lois G. Forer — *Unequal Protection: Women, Children, and the Elderly in Court*. New York: Norton, 1991.

Lawrence M. Friedman — *Crime and Punishment in American History*. New York: BasicBooks, 1993.

Hiroshi Fukurai, Edgar W. Butler, and Richard Krooth — *Race and the Jury: Racial Disenfranchisement and the Search for Justice*. New York: Plenum Press, 1993.

Russell W. Galloway   *Justice for All? The Rich and Poor in Supreme Court History, 1790–1990*. Durham, NC: Carolina Academic Press, 1991.

Mary Ann Glendon   *A Nation Under Lawyers: How the Crisis in the Legal Profession Is Transforming American Society*. New York: Farrar, Straus & Giroux, 1994.

Roy Grutman and Bill Thomas   *Lawyers and Thieves*. New York: Simon and Schuster, 1990.

Mona Harrington   *Women Lawyers: Rewriting the Rules*. New York: Knopf, 1993.

Eugene W. Hickok and Gary L. McDowell   *Justice vs. Law: Courts and Politics in American Society*. New York: Free Press, 1993.

Philip K. Howard   *The Death of Common Sense: How Law Is Suffocating America*. New York: Random House, 1994.

Peter W. Huber   *Galileo's Revenge: Junk Science in the Courtroom*. New York: BasicBooks, 1991.

Peter W. Huber and Robert E. Litan, eds.   *The Liability Maze: The Impact of Liability Law on Safety and Innovation*. Washington, DC: Brookings Institution, 1991.

Robert E. Litan, ed.   *Verdict: Assessing the Civil Jury System*. Washington, DC: Brookings Institution, 1993.

David W. Marston   *Malice Aforethought: How Lawyers Use Our Secret Rules to Get Rich, Get Sex, Get Even . . . and Get Away with It*. New York: Morrow, 1991.

Richard W. Moll   *The Lure of the Law*. New York: Viking, 1990.

Robert F. Nagel   *Judicial Power and American Character: Censoring Ourselves in an Anxious Age*. New York: Oxford University Press, 1994.

Polly Nelson   *Defending the Devil: My Story as Ted Bundy's Last Lawyer*. New York: Morrow, 1994.

Walter K. Olson   *The Litigation Explosion: What Happened When America Unleashed the Lawsuit*. New York: Truman Talley Books/Dutton, 1991.

Brian J. Ostrom and Neal B. Kauder   "Examining the Work of State Courts, 1993: A National Perspective from the Court Statistics Project." Monograph, NCSC Publications, Williamsburg, VA, 1993.

Susanne A. Roschwalb and Richard A. Stack, eds.   *Litigation Public Relations: Courting Public Opinion*. Littleton, CO: Fred B. Rothman, 1995.

Paula S. Rothenberg   *Race, Class, and Gender in the United States: An Integrated Study*. 2nd ed. New York: St. Martin's Press, 1992.

Michael Rustad   "Demystifying Punitive Damages in Products Liability Cases: A Survey of a Quarter Century of Trial Verdicts." Paper, Roscoe Pound Foundation, Washington, DC, 1991.

Robert Satter   *Doing Justice: A Trial Judge at Work*. New York: American Lawyer Books/Simon and Schuster, 1990.

Thomas L. Shaffer with Mary M. Shaffer   *American Lawyers and Their Communities: Ethics in the Legal Profession*. Notre Dame, IN: University of Notre Dame Press, 1991.

Christopher E. Smith   *Courts and the Poor*. Chicago: Nelson-Hall, 1991.

Linda Thurston, ed.   *A Call to Action: An Analysis and Overview of the United States Criminal Justice System*. Chicago: Third World Press, 1993.

Index

Schwartz, Victor, 59, 61
Scottsboro Boys case, 132
Senate Committees. *See under* United
    States
sentencing, 127, 130
  current leniency of, 138
  mandatory minimum
    is fair, 137-40
      con, 141-46
    is supported by public, 139
  racism of, 129, 134-35
  victims should be present during,
    156
    con, 160-61
Sentencing Commission, The, 145
Shannon, James M., 129
Shaw, David, 181
Shively, Jill, 191
Simon, Rita J., 177, 183
Simpson, O.J. *See* O.J. Simpson case
Smith, William Kennedy, case of, 46,
    172, 190
Snyder, Harry, 97, 98
Sotello, Johnny, 152
Sowell, Thomas, 23
Spayd, Liz, 56
Spencer, Betty Jane, 156
St. John, Dale, 195
St. Paul Pioneer Press, 176, 179
Stanford Law School, 199
State Farm Insurance, 108
Stewart, Julie, 145
Stewart, Larry S., 85
Strauss, Marcy, 45
Strossen, Nadine, 148, 149, 150

Tans, M., 178
Terenzio, John, 198
Time magazine, 112, 189
Toobin, Jeffrey, 183
tort system
  benefits of, 82, 121
  caseload is increasing, 57
    con, 106, 120
  and difficulty of proof, 73
  encourages safer products, 85
  hinders medical research, 78
  is expensive in U.S., 92, 93
  is inefficient, 60, 115
  is under attack, 95
  needs meaningful reform, 79, 109,
    110, 116
  see also litigation explosion; loser
    pays rule
Towers Perrin, 60
trial lawyers, 61, 66, 70, 92
  of O.J. Simpson, 201
  unpopular with corporations, 65

trials
  have always been public, 167, 170
  televising of,
    demeans justice, 171-74
    is public right, 166-70
  see also crime victims; publicity
TRXO Production v. Alliance Resources,
    84
Twain, Mark, 36
Twerski, Aaron, 79
Tyrrell, R. Emmett, Jr., 90
Tyson, Mike, 41

United States, 23, 24, 36, 121
  commitment to individual rights,
    119
  Congress, 32, 37, 58, 145, 158
    Republican-led, 59, 72
  Constitution, 156
    First Amendment, 46, 49, 50, 52,
      187
    Fourth Amendment, 167
    Sixth Amendment, 157-58
    Seventh Amendment, 27, 31, 32,
      34
    should be repealed, 37
  Court of Appeals, 34
  Department of Justice, 103, 120, 140
  Founding Fathers of, 24, 29, 156,
    172
  Navy, 113, 114
  Senate Committee on Commerce,
    Science, and Transportation, 76,
    78, 79, 81, 84
  Senate Committee on
    Governmental Affairs, 76
  Supreme Court, 32, 35, 43, 49, 129
    on civil forfeiture, 148, 149
    and death penalty, 145
    and *Florida Star v. B.J.F.*, 41
    is to blame for checkbook
      journalism, 198
    on punitive damages, 84
    and sentencing, 144, 145
    should be televised, 168
United States v. Park, 149
unsafe products, 63, 65-66, 121
  versus individual responsibility,
    102-104, 115
  see also asbestos; McDonald's/
    Lieberman case
USA Today, 127
U.S. News & World Report, 102

Victim and Witness Protection Act
  (1982), 160
victims. *See* crime victims
Vincent, James, 78

209